BEEF UP
Your
BRAIN

The BIG BOOK of 301 Brain-Building Exercises, Puzzles, and Games

Michel Noir, Ph.D. & Bernard Croisile, M.D., Ph.D.

New York Chicago San Francisco Lisbon London Madrid Mexico City
Milan New Delhi San Juan Seoul Singapore Sydney Toronto

Library of Congress Cataloging-in-Publication Data

Noir, Michel, 1944–
    Beef up your brain : the big book of 301 brain-building exercises, puzzles, and
games / Michel Noir and Bernard Croisile.
        p.   cm.
    ISBN-10: 0-07-170058-7 (alk. paper)
    ISBN-13: 978-0-07-170058-0 (alk. paper)
    1. Intellect—Problems, exercises, etc.   2. Logic puzzles.   I. Croisile,
Bernard.   II. Title.

BF431.3.N647 2010
    153—dc22   2009035657

1 2 3 4 5 6 7 8 9 10 11 12 13 14 15 16 17 18 19   FGR/FGR   0 9

ISBN 978-0-07-170058-0
MHID   0-07-170058-7

McGraw-Hill books are available at special quantity discounts to use as premiums and
sales promotions or for use in corporate training programs. To contact a representative
please e-mail us at bulksales@mcgraw-hill.com.

Contents

Introduction

Does Your Brain Need Beefing Up?

The human brain is one of the most complex organisms known. When working at optimum levels, it can process loads of data as quickly as a computer. Although a computer's hard drive can ultimately store much more data, our brains can store "data" in ways that a computer never could— instantly recalling how crème brûlée smells, feels, and tastes when this dessert is mentioned. Unfortunately the brain doesn't always remain working at optimum levels . . . unless you work on it!

More and more, scientific evidence is proving that our minds don't *have* to deteriorate as they age. There are preventive measures we can take that will significantly increase the probability of staying mentally and physically fit throughout our lives. This is good news of course, because mental fitness and agility translate to an enhanced quality of life. Physical exercise, good nutrition, social connection with others, and mental stimulation all play important roles in ensuring that our brains remain sharp and agile at any age.

Scientists the world over have been doing research for decades on how some people can stay "with it" while others cannot. The Advanced Cognitive Training for Independent and Vital Elderly (ACTIVE) study, funded by the National Institutes of Health, demonstrated recently that older adults could improve their cognitive abilities with proper training and that some of these gains could be maintained several years later. In this experiment conducted by a number of researchers, more than 2,800 adults aged 65 to 94 received training in memory, reasoning, or processing speed. After about ten hours of training, each group improved significantly in the area in which they were trained. Even five years later subjects maintained many of their improvements.

Research on the physical results of thinking hard—as one is bound to do when solving a puzzle—has shown that just using the brain actually expands the links that interconnect brain cells. The more we think, the better our brains function . . . regardless of age. The renowned brain researcher Dr. Marian Diamond says,

"The nervous system possesses not just a 'morning' of flexibility, but an 'afternoon' and an 'evening' as well." Dr. Diamond found that whether we are young or old, we can continue to broaden our minds. The brain can change at any age.

Other studies reveal that physical health is a key component of mental health, too. According to research published in the *British Journal of Sports Medicine*, brain power decline can be prevented and possibly even reversed by engaging in regular aerobic exercise. Leading cognitive neuroscientists Art Kramer (U.S. Beckman Institute at the University of Illinois) and Kirk Erickson (University of Pittsburgh) offer a critical evaluation of the large number of studies that show how aerobic exercise and physical activity can be beneficial to the aging brain.

The expression "use it or lose it" applies to muscles in our bodies as well as to neural pathways and connections in our brains. And what is more exhilarating than learning something new at every stage of our lives? Scientists all over the world agree that the evidence is now overwhelming: mentally stimulating lives beef up your brain power. Numerous landmark studies have found that engaging in mentally stimulating activities throughout our lives can help keep our minds sharp. Several of the studies cite participating in challenging, interactive games as one effective method to keep the brain challenged and agile, and several studies look specifically at targeted skills training. That's why we've put together *Beef Up Your Brain*—every time you do some of the puzzles in this generously portioned book, it's like taking your brain to the gym.

So suit up, and let's get started!

Easy
Puzzles

No Pain, No _____

Can you supply the beginning words of each of the following proverbs?

1. _____ is another man's gain.

2. _____ louder than words.

3. _____ losers weepers.

No Pain, No _____

Can you supply the beginning words of each of the following proverbs?

1. ___Silence_____ is golden.

2. _____ is human.

3. _____ those who help themselves.

No Pain, No _____

Can you supply the beginning words of each of the following proverbs?

1. _____ saves nine.

2. _____ is believing.

3. _____ the mother of all wisdom.

No Pain, No _____

Can you supply the beginning words of each of the following proverbs?

1. _____ like son.

2. _____ to godliness.

3. _____ the heart is.

Entangled Figures

Examine the figure below; then determine which three of the nine figures below it are combined to form the figure.

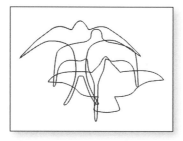

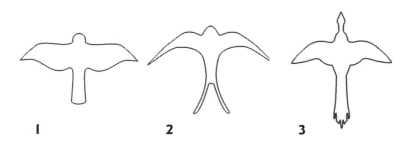

1

2

3

4

5

6

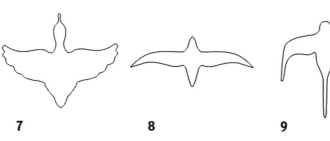

7

8

9

Entangled Figures

Examine the figure below; then determine which three of the nine figures below it are combined to form the figure.

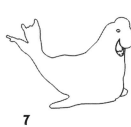

1

2

3

4

5

6

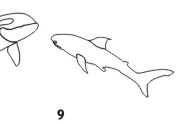

7

8

9

Entangled Figures

Examine the figure below; then determine which three of the nine figures below it are combined to form the figure.

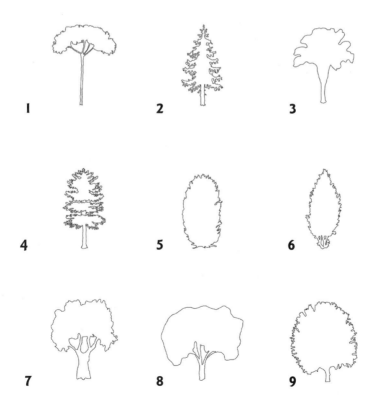

All-Star Game

Of the nine words below, only six can be placed in the star. Arrows indicate the direction in which each word is placed. To assist you, one letter has already been placed in the star.

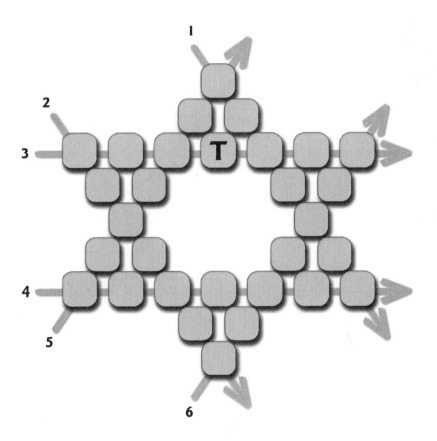

EXHAUST	CONTACT
COTTAGE	TRACHEA
SPATULA	TETANUS
WATTAGE	SUCCESS
EYEBROW	

All-Star Game

Of the nine words below, only six can be placed in the star. Arrows indicate the direction in which each word is placed. To assist you, one letter has already been placed in the star.

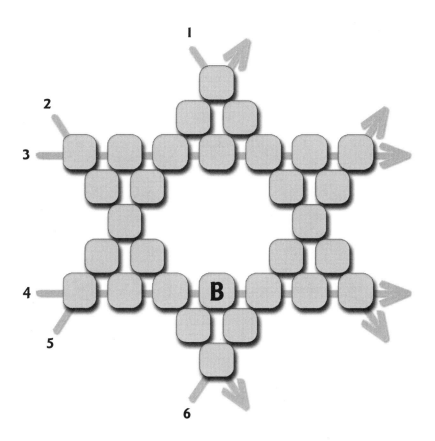

SUAVITY   MYSTERY

MINIBUS   CABBAGE

ALEWIFE   CANASTA

WEATHER   DOUBTER

SPRAYER

All-Star Game

Of the nine words below, only six can be placed in the star. Arrows indicate the direction in which each word is placed. To assist you, one letter has already been placed in the star.

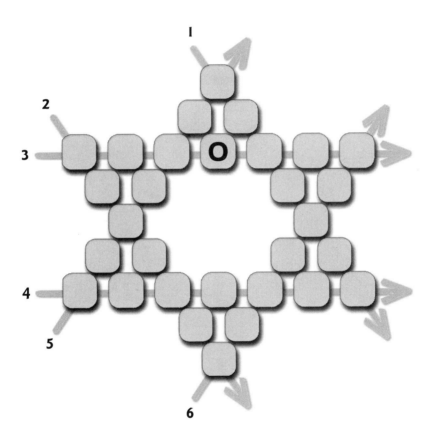

CORONER

REVERIE

HEATHER

WHISPER

INVOICE

RELAPSE

HEROINE

SCHOLAR

SPARROW

All-Star Game

Of the nine words below, only six can be placed in the star. Arrows indicate the direction in which each word is placed. To assist you, one letter has already been placed in the star.

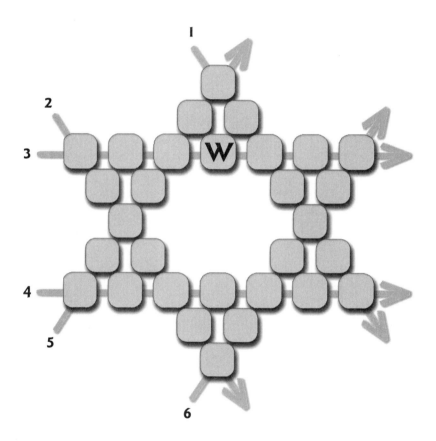

PLOWING	SURFACE
SOILAGE	ALEWIFE
TRAINER	AERIALS
PRAIRIE	SKIMMER
PARSECS	

Towers of Hanoi

Determine the fewest number of moves necessary to change the configuration in Figure A to that shown in Figure B. You may not place a larger disk on a smaller one, and you may move only one disk at a time.

A

B

Towers of Hanoi

Determine the fewest number of moves necessary to change the configuration in Figure A to that shown in Figure B. You may not place a larger disk on a smaller one, and you may move only one disk at a time.

A

B

Towers of Hanoi

Determine the fewest number of moves necessary to change the configuration in Figure A to that shown in Figure B. You may not place a larger disk on a smaller one, and you may move only one disk at a time.

A

B

Easy as One-Two-Three

Take a careful look at the figure below and count the number of squares it has.

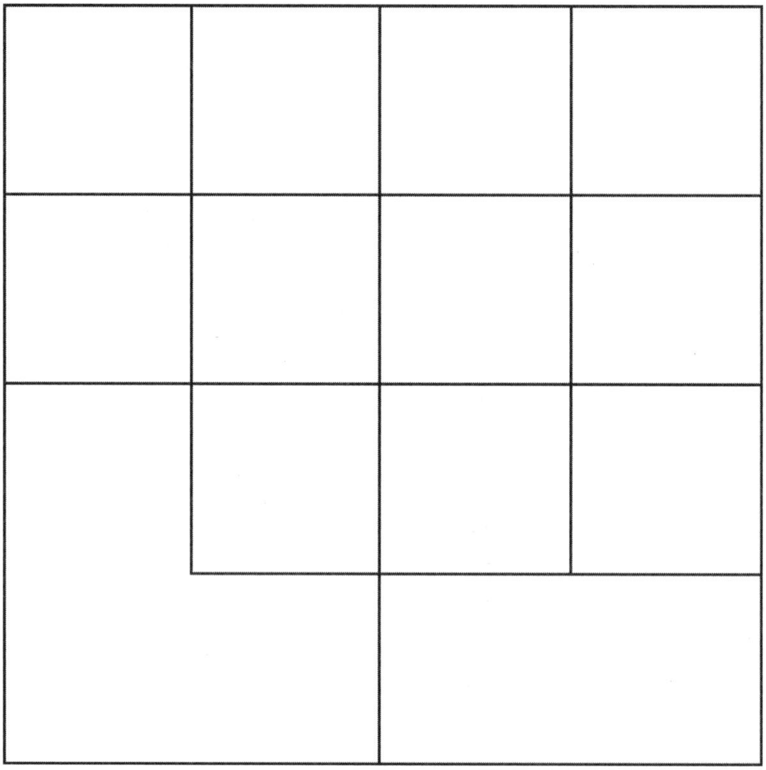

Easy as One-Two-Three

Take a careful look at the figure below and count the number of squares it has.

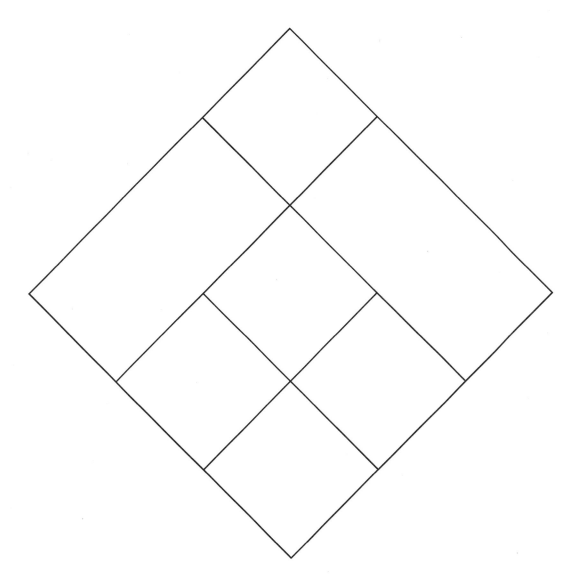

Easy as One-Two-Three

Take a careful look at the figure below and count the number of squares it has.

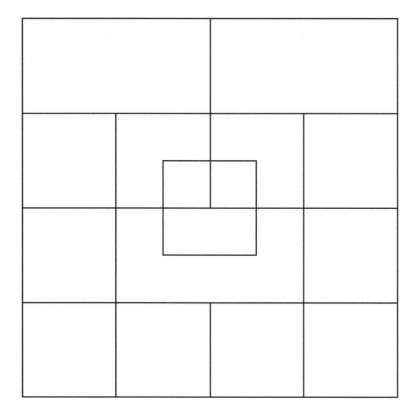

Can You Spot Me?

Find the odd one in this series.

✳✳✳✳✳✳✳✳✳✳✳✳✳✳✳✳✳✳✳✳✳✳✳✳✳✳✳✳✳✳✳✳
✳✳✳✳✳✳✳✳✳✳✳✳✳✳✳✳✳✳✳✳✳✳✳✳✳✳✳✳✳✳✳✳
✳✳✳✳✳✳✳✳✳✳✳✳✳✳✳✳✳✳✳✳✳✳✳✳✳✳✳✳✳✳✳✳
✳✳✳✳✳✳✳✳✳✳✳✳✳✳✳✳✳✳✳✳✳✳✳✳✳✳✳✳✳✳✳✳
✳✳✳✳✳✳✳✳✳✳✳✳✳✳✳✳✳✳✳✳✳✳✳✳✳✳✳✳✳✳✳✳

HINT: *the odd one is* ✴

Can You Spot Me?

Find the odd one in this series.

XXXXXXXXXXXXXXXXXXXXXXXXXXXXXXXXXXXXXXXX
XXXXXXXXXXXXXXXXXXXXXXXXXXXXXXXXXXXXXXXX
XXXXXXXXXXXXXXXXXXXXXXXXXXXXXXXXXXXXXXXX
XXXXXXXXXXXXXXXXXXXXXXXXXXXXXXXXXXXXXXXX
XXXXXXXXXXXXXXXXXXXXXXXXXXXXXXXXXXXXXXXX

HINT: *the odd one is* ✗

Can You Spot Me?

Find the odd one in this series.

O'O'O'O'O'O'O'O'O'O'O'O'O'O'O'O'O'O'O'O'O'O'O'
O'O'O'O'O'O'O'O'O'O'O'O'O'O'O'O'O'O'O'O'O'O'O'
O'O'O'O'O'O'O'O'O'O'O'O'O'O'O'O'O'O'O'O'O'O'O'
O'O'O'O'O'O'O'O'O'O'O'O'O'O'O'O'O'O'O'O'O'O O'
O'O'O'O'O'O'O'O'O'O'O'O'O'O'O'O'O'O'O'O'O'O'O'

HINT: *the odd one is* O

Warming Up

Read the text below and write down all of the "sh" sounds.

She was so deceptive that no one could guess she was actually cheating all the time, and that her prudish looks hid shameful behaviors that only she knew. She was capable of going to church and confessing the most hideous sins to the priest without feeling ashamed. Her friends were quite sure she was of an honest nature, and that she was a perfect match with Andy, the charming boy whom all the young ladies fell for.

Warming Up

Read the text below and write down all of the "f" sounds.

Bob drank his coffee then silently prayed for things to go smoothly. He felt the easy phase of bringing the girl back home was just the first step of many harder ones, and that if she did not feel safe here, she would flee once again, with only a few chances to find her quickly. This was a rough world, and the pictures of the happy days that should have brought joy to his fear-stricken heart could not help much.

Incomplete Workout

Which of the three tiles below completes the picture?

I	2	3

Incomplete Workout

Which of the three tiles below completes the picture?

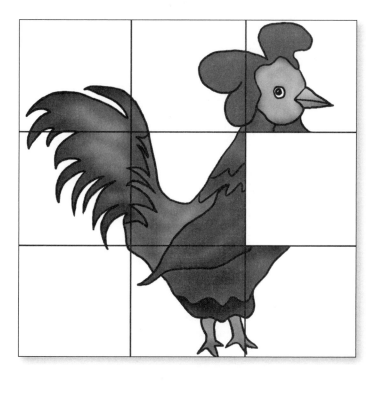

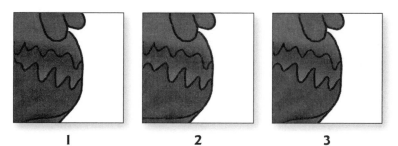

1   2   3

Hidden Strength

Find the ten words hidden in the grid. They can be read horizontally, vertically, or diagonally; backward or forward; up or down. The same letter can be used in several different words.

HINT: *the theme is* **music**.

```
Z  E  D  E  N  K  D  K  Y  S  K  B
C  B  C  V  S  L  Z  G  P  M  E  S
T  E  B  S  Y  L  T  P  M  E  E  D
E  A  L  C  Z  N  U  M  Z  L  R  F
R  B  Z  L  S  Y  M  P  H  O  N  Y
P  S  V  I  O  L  I  N  N  D  D  F
R  D  F  Z  N  G  B  H  B  Y  N  T
E  S  F  B  A  N  D  B  G  P  N  Z
T  R  H  Y  T  H  M  N  U  S  A  A
N  B  J  H  A  T  W  L  O  O  L  Z
I  D  D  F  R  T  S  D  V  C  P  N
W  X  S  S  A  R  G  E  U  L  B  X
```

Hidden Strength

Find the ten words hidden in the grid. They can be read horizontally, vertically, or diagonally; backward or forward; up or down. The same letter can be used in several different words.

HINT: *the theme is* **food**.

G	H	F	Y	G	B	U	I	L	V	N	Z
G	S	F	Q	H	K	S	A	D	F	E	Y
C	V	E	K	N	R	F	X	D	R	B	K
A	V	V	L	E	F	A	D	B	G	C	N
D	A	E	R	B	O	N	I	O	N	Z	S
H	A	G	V	B	A	U	C	X	W	B	S
Q	T	G	B	Z	J	T	S	N	L	M	Y
C	S	I	Z	S	H	O	E	J	I	K	C
D	A	I	S	N	H	M	Z	G	M	R	H
X	P	F	G	H	M	A	I	Z	E	C	B
Z	V	H	Y	J	K	T	D	B	E	V	S
Z	B	A	D	L	I	O	D	F	B	E	Z

Working Both Sides

Take a careful look at these two sets of characters. Which characters appear in the series on the right but not in the series on the left?

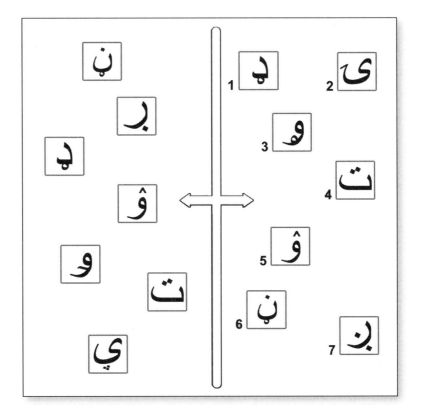

Working Both Sides

Take a careful look at these two sets of characters. Which characters appear in the series on the right but not in the series on the left?

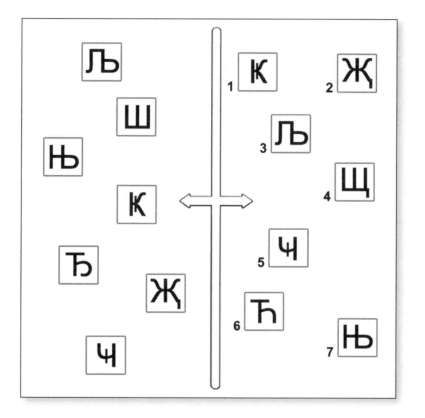

The Circuit Workout

Try to find the logical order of the pictures below.

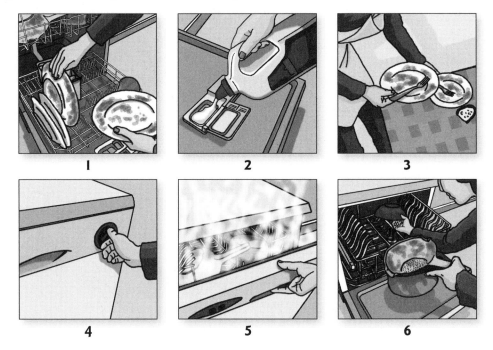

It Takes Two

Which two geishas are exactly alike?

It Takes Two

Which two birds are exactly alike?

Pencils Up

Link the twelve stars with sixteen branches without raising your pencil.
You cannot touch the other figures, and you cannot go between two
figures more than once.

Pencils Up

Link the twelve hexagonal figures without raising your pencil. You cannot touch the other figures, and you cannot go between two figures more than once.

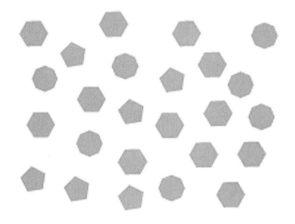

Spinning Class

Determine whether the two figures below are identical or mirror images.

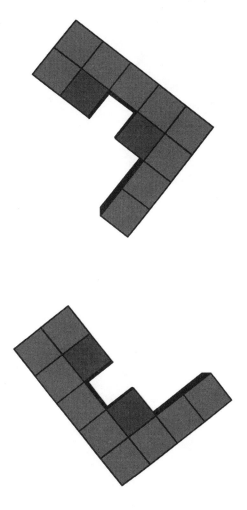

Spinning Class

Determine whether the two figures below are identical or mirror images.

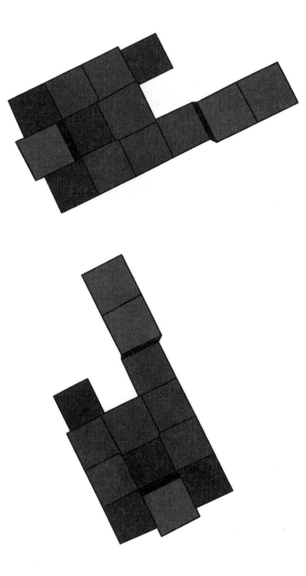

Resistance Training

Find the odd word in the following series, and justify your answer.

Big Ben	British Museum	Westminster Abbey	Rockefeller Center	Tower Bridge

The odd one is: _____

spade	scalpel	rake	pruning shears	trowel

The odd one is: _____

Resistance Training

Find the odd word in the following series, and justify your answer.

Michael Schumacher	Richard Hamilton	Tony Parker	Kevin Garnett	Paul Pierce

The odd one is: _____

Sun	Mars	Mercury	Venus	Jupiter

The odd one is: _____

Resistance Training

Find the odd word in the following series, and justify your answer.

snail	crayfish	lobster	shrimp	crab

The odd one is: _____

Diamonds Are a Girl's Best Friend	Two Little Girls from Little Rock	Some Like It Hot	The Wall	River of No Return

The odd one is: _____

Resistance Training

Find the odd word in the following series, and justify your answer.

beef	pork	cod	mutton	veal

The odd one is: _____

beech	oak	willow	fir	poplar

The odd one is: _____

Resistance Training

Find the odd word in the following series, and justify your answer.

D. H. Lawrence	F. Scott Fitzgerald	Oscar Wilde	Charles Dickens	Tom Cruise

The odd one is: _____

France	Morocco	Great Britain	Spain	Italy

The odd one is: _____

Power Squats

Find a seven-letter word in the grid below. The first two letters are shown in the shaded squares. Letters must be adjacent to the next letter in the word.

C	S	M	A
F	**U**	R	L
S	R	E	L
B	R	I	I

Power Squats

Find a seven-letter word in the grid below. The first two letters are shown in the shaded squares. Letters must be adjacent to the next letter in the word.

T	E	F	H
O	U	D	L
R	R	I	E
A	I	S	M

Power Squats

Find an eight-letter word in the grid below. The first two letters are shown in the shaded squares. Letters must be adjacent to the next letter in the word.

B	**P**	P	E
U	**R**	O	R
L	D	I	T
M	I	V	y

Power Squats

Find an eight-letter word in the grid below. The first two letters are shown in the shaded squares. Letters must be adjacent to the next letter in the word.

D	S	I	M
L	T	**O**	**M**
R	U	N	S
E	U	E	I

Power Squats

Find an eight-letter word in the grid below. The first two letters are shown in the shaded squares. Letters must be adjacent to the next letter in the word.

S	E	C	B
S	S	N	L
D	**R**	I	O
E	**P**	T	U

Power Squats

Find a seven-letter word in the grid below. The first two letters are shown in the shaded squares. Letters must be adjacent to the next letter in the word.

A	R	P	R
N	C	H	I
G	Y	L	V
O	N	E	E

Power Squats

Find a seven-letter word in the grid below. The first two letters are shown in the shaded squares. Letters must be adjacent to the next letter in the word.

P	T	I	L
E	**R**	N	E
S	O	I	G
S	B	A	R

Power Squats

Find a seven-letter word in the grid below. The first two letters are shown in the shaded squares. Letters must be adjacent to the next letter in the word.

C	S	P	H
O	A	N	Y
M	P	E	I
A	L	R	E

The Proper Form

Among the hands below, find the right hands and the left hands.

| 1 | 2 | 3 |

The Proper Form

Among the hands below, find the right hands and the left hands.

1   2   3

The Proper Form

Among the hands below, find the right hands and the left hands.

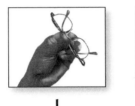

I	2	3

The Proper Form

Among the hands below, find the right hands and the left hands.

1   2   3

The Proper Form

Among the hands below, find the right hands and the left hands.

I	2	3

The Proper Form

Among the hands below, find the right hands and the left hands.

1   2   3

The Proper Form

Among the hands below, find the right hands and the left hands.

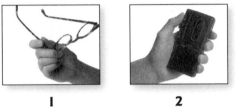

| 1 | 2 | 3 |

The Proper Form

Among the hands below, find the right hands and the left hands.

1

2

3

Muscle Memory

Match each actor with the movie in which he or she starred.

1. Tom Cruise

2. Tom Hanks

3. Jodie Foster

4. Leonor Watling

5. Sylvester Stallone

A. *Forrest Gump*

B. *Talk to Her*

C. *Top Gun*

D. *Rambo*

E. *The Silence of the Lambs*

Muscle Memory

Match each state with its capital.

1. Hawaii   **A.** Austin

2. Arizona   **B.** Denver

3. Texas   **C.** Phoenix

4. Virginia   **D.** Honolulu

5. Colorado   **E.** Richmond

Muscle Memory

Match each animal with the animal group to which it belongs.

1. turtle   **A.** fish

2. cow   **B.** bird

3. vulture   **C.** insect

4. trout   **D.** reptile

5. honey bee   **E.** mammal

Muscle Memory

Match each monument with the city in which it is located.

1. Statue of Liberty   **A.** San Francisco

2. Eiffel Tower   **B.** New York

3. Big Ben   **C.** Montreal

4. Golden Gate Bridge   **D.** London

5. Pont Jacques Cartier   **E.** Paris

Working Both Sides

Take a careful look at these two sets of characters. Which characters appear in the series on the right but not in the series on the left?

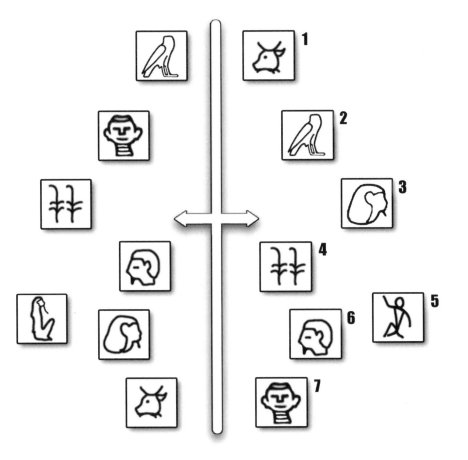

Working Both Sides

Take a careful look at these two sets of characters. Which characters appear in the series on the right but not in the series on the left?

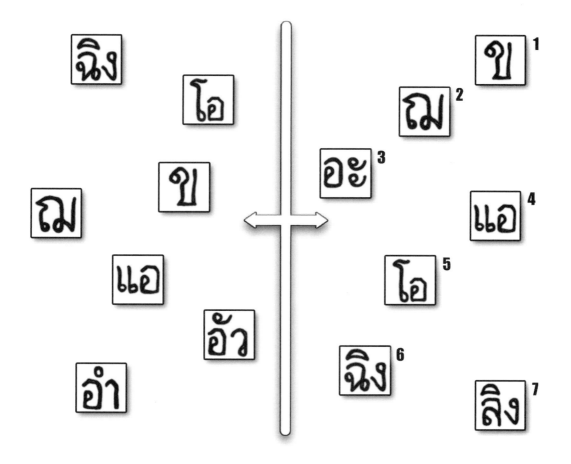

Interval Training

Can you form ten two-part words from the fragments below? Each part can be used only once, and the splits may not necessarily be the part splits you find in the dictionary.

HINT: *The theme is* **clothes**.

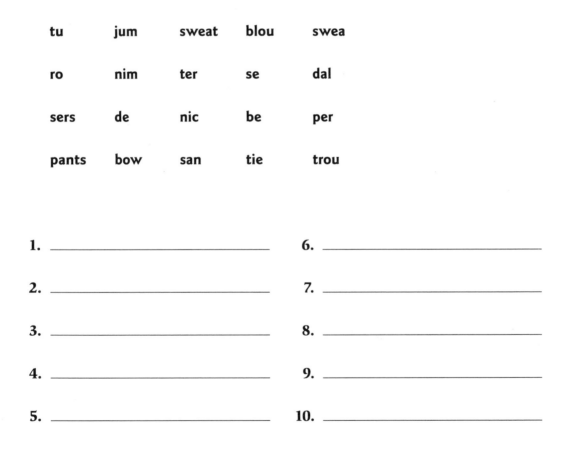

tu	jum	sweat	blou	swea
ro	nim	ter	se	dal
sers	de	nic	be	per
pants	bow	san	tie	trou

1. _____   6. _____

2. _____   7. _____

3. _____   8. _____

4. _____   9. _____

5. _____   10. _____

Interval Training

Can you form ten two-part words from the fragments below? Each part can be used only once, and the splits may not necessarily be the part splits you find in the dictionary.

HINT: *The theme is* **clothes**.

cho	cking	gar	ve	tten
cket	pon	coat	rain	ja
ment	co	mi	sto	suit
glo	swim	ckers	kni	llar

1. _____   6. _____

2. _____   7. _____

3. _____   8. _____

4. _____   9. _____

5. _____   10. _____

Interval Training

Can you form ten two-part words from the fragments below? Each part can be used only once, and the splits may not necessarily be the part splits you find in the dictionary.

HINT: *The theme is* **dance.**

tan	tu	sa	lo	sal
pol	rhy	rum	llet	trot
ba	ka	go	thm	tu
bo	fox-	mam	so	ba

1. _____   6. _____

2. _____   7. _____

3. _____   8. _____

4. _____   9. _____

5. _____   10. _____

Interval Training

Can you form ten two-part words from the fragments below? Each part can be used only once, and the splits may not necessarily be the part splits you find in the dictionary.

HINT: *The theme is* **dance.**

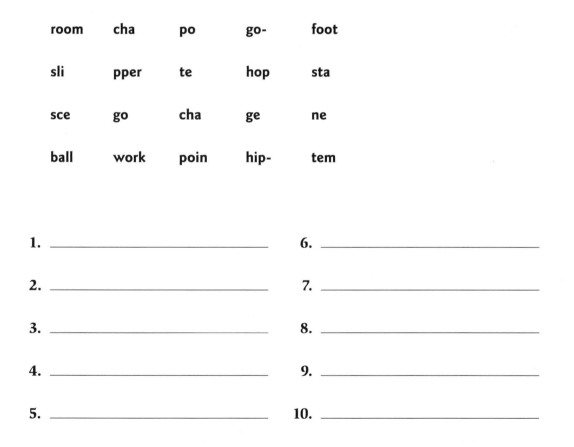

room	cha	po	go-	foot
sli	pper	te	hop	sta
sce	go	cha	ge	ne
ball	work	poin	hip-	tem

1. _____   6. _____

2. _____   7. _____

3. _____   8. _____

4. _____   9. _____

5. _____   10. _____

Combination Sets

Take a careful look at the four elements below and try to determine which ones are not part of the larger figure. Beware, some elements may just have been turned around.

1   2   3   4

Combination Sets

Take a careful look at the four elements below and try to determine
which ones are not part of the larger figure. Beware, some elements may
just have been turned around.

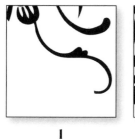

1

2

3

4

Distance Run

Take a careful look at the location of the five objects in this landscape.

The image below shows the same landscape as seen from above. Determine where you would stand in the scenery to view the landscape as it appears in the image above.

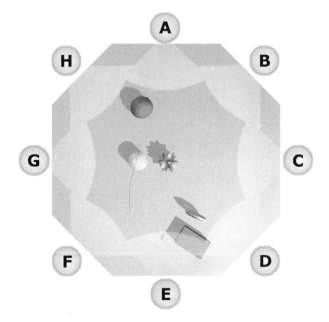

Distance Run

Take a careful look at the location of the five objects in this landscape.

The image below shows the same landscape as seen from above. Determine where you would stand in the scenery to view the landscape as it appears in the image above.

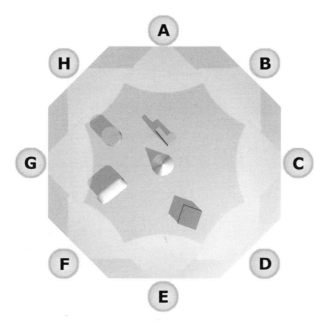

Cross Training

Decipher this quotation from Oscar Wilde. Each symbol represents a letter, but it is always the same letter.

HINT: *Vowels are represented in the light gray squares.*

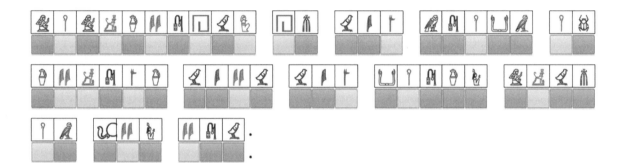

Cross Training

Decipher this quotation from Winston Churchill. Each symbol represents a letter, but it is always the same letter.

HINT: *Vowels are represented in the light gray squares.*

Cross Training

Decipher this quotation from Jane Wagner. Each symbol represents a letter, but it is always the same letter.

HINT: *Vowels are represented in the light gray squares.*

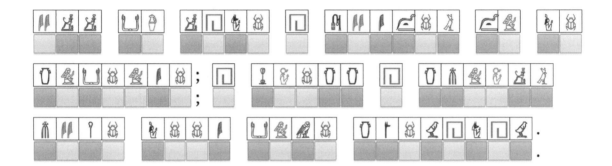

Cross Training

Decipher this quotation from Norman Mailer. Each symbol represents a letter, but it is always the same letter.

HINT: *Vowels are represented in the light gray squares.*

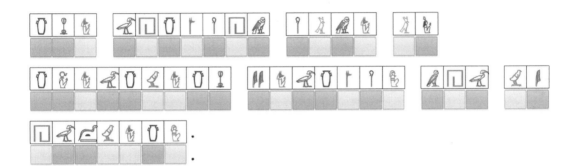

Reverse Crunches

Find the opposite of each of the words below. The first letter has been given as a clue.

1. beautiful: u_____

2. rich: p_____

3. close: o_____

Which word is not a synonym of the other four?

weird   uncanny   problematic   strange   unusual

Reverse Crunches

Find the opposite of each of the words below. The first letter has been given as a clue.

1. long: s_____

2. discreet: i_____

3. forbidden: a_____

Which word is not a synonym of the other four?

consider   reflect on   ponder   think   tell

Reverse Crunches

Find the opposite of each of the words below. The first letter has been given as a clue.

1. true: f_____

2. accept: r_____

3. admirable: d_____

Which word is not a synonym of the other four?

    manufacture   make   create   produce   meditate

Reverse Crunches

Find the opposite of each of the words below. The first letter has been given as a clue.

1. small: b_____

2. raw: c_____

3. complicate: s_____

Which word is not a synonym of the other four?

celebrated   famed   famous   renowned   tranquil

Reverse Crunches

Find the opposite of each of the words below. The first letter has been given as a clue.

1. busy: i_____

2. easy: h_____

3. careful: c_____

Which word is not a synonym of the other four?

elastic　　**rigid**　　**flexible**　　**pliable**　　**pliant**

Reverse Crunches

Find the opposite of each of the words below. The first letter has been given as a clue.

1. increasing: d_____

2. empty: f_____

3. less: m_____

Which word is not a synonym of the other four?

fate   pride   destiny   fortune   luck

Maxing Out

Identify the six differences between these two pictures.

Maxing Out

Identify the six differences between these two pictures.

Working the Memory Muscle

Take a minute to memorize the six words below without looking at the bottom half of the page.

shrimp

cow

cupboard

design

elephant

part

Now cover up the list of words and answer the following questions:

1. What, if any, animals are on the list?

_____

2. Name the abstract words on the list.

_____

3. Which word is the shortest on the list?

_____

Working the Memory Muscle

Take a minute to memorize the six words below without looking at the bottom half of the page.

tea

document

feather

happiness

chef

certainty

Now cover up the list of words and answer the following questions:

1. Which drink is on the list?

_____

2. What, if any, profession is on the list?

_____

3. Which word from the list can be found on a bird?

_____

Can You Spot Me?

Find the odd one in this series.

hhhhhhhhhhhhhhhhhhhhhhhhhhhhhhhhhhhhhhhhhhhhhhhhhhhhhhhhhhhhhh
hhhhhhhhhhhhhhhhhhhhhhhhhhhhhhhhhhhhhhhhhhhhhhhhhhhhhhhhhhhhhh
hhhhhhhhhnhhhhhhhhhhhhhhhhhhhhhhhhhhhhhhhhhhhhhhhhhhhhhhhhhhhhh
hhhhhhhhhhhhhhhhhhhhhhhhhhhhhhhhhhhhhhhhhhhhhhhhhhhhhhhhhhhhhh
hhhhhhhhhhhhhhhhhhhhhhhhhhhhhhhhhhhhhhhhhhhhhhhhhhhhhhhhhhhhhh
hhhhhhhhhhhhhhhhhhhhhhhhhhhhhhhhhhhhhhhhhhhhhhhhhhhhhhhhhhhhhh

HINT: *The odd one is* **n.**

Can You Spot Me?

Find the odd one in this series.

èè
èè
èèèèèèèèèèèèèèèèèèèèéèèè
èè
èè
èè

HINT: *The odd one is* **é**.

Can You Spot Me?

Find the odd one in this series.

RRRRRRRRRRRRRRRRRRRRRRRRRRRRRRRRRRRRRRRRRRRRRRRRRRR
RRRRRRRRRRRRRRRRRRRRRRRRRRRRRRRRRRRRRRRRRRRRRRRRRRR
RRRRRRRRRRRRRRRRRRRRRRRRRRRRRRRRRRRRRRRRRRRRRRRRRRR
RRRRRRRRRRRRRRRRRRRRRRRRRRRRRRRRRRRRRRRRRRRRRRRRRRR
RRRRRRRRRRRRRRRRRRRRRRRRRRRRRRRRRRRRRRRRRRRRRRRRRRR
RRRPRRRRRRRRRRRRRRRRRRRRRRRRRRRRRRRRRRRRRRRRRRRRRRR

HINT: *The odd one is* **P.**

Can You Spot Me?

Find the odd one in this series.

HINT: *The odd one is* 🥟.

Can You Spot Me?

Find the odd one in this series.

↩↩↩
↩↩↩
↩↩↩
↩↩↩
↩←↩↩↩↩↩↩↩↩↩↩↩↩↩↩↩↩↩↩↩↩↩↩↩↩↩↩↩↩↩↩↩↩↩↩↩↩↩↩↩
↩↩↩

HINT: *The odd one is* ←.

Can You Spot Me?

Find the odd one in this series.

HINT: *The odd one is* ❤.

Can You Spot Me?

Find the odd one in this series.

HINT: *The odd one is* ⊻ .

Cooling Down

Are the following statements right or wrong?

1. Spiders are insects.

2. *Moby-Dick* was written by Herman Melville.

3. Christmas is on December 26.

4. Tees are accessories to play golf.

5. Christopher Columbus was Italian.

Cooling Down

Are the following statements right or wrong?

1. The chemical symbol for silver is Ag.

2. Thailand is a European country.

3. Mark Knopfler is a member of the Rolling Stones.

4. Tiger Woods is a golf player.

5. The flag of Great Britain has five colors.

Cooling Down

Are the following statements right or wrong?

1. Marilyn Monroe played in the movie *Some Like It Hot.*

2. The approximate value of pi is 3.1416.

3. Some inhabitants of Germany are called Hamburgers.

4. Virginia Woolf was American.

5. Fur is made of animal skins.

Cooling Down

Are the following statements right or wrong?

1. Montreal is the capital of Canada.

2. John F. Kennedy was born in 1920.

3. Britney Spears wrote "Like a Virgin."

4. Brazil and Bolivia have a common border.

5. Cathedrals are Catholic churches.

Cooling Down

Are the following statements right or wrong?

1. *Romeo and Juliet* was written by Shakespeare.

2. Katrina was a hurricane.

3. The Koran is the holy book for the Jews.

4. Roses can be black.

5. Squares have four sides.

Cooling Down

Are the following statements right or wrong?

1. Leukemia is a skin disease.

2. Margaret Thatcher was a prime minister in Ireland.

3. Alaska is a state of the USA.

4. Highlands are mountains of Switzerland.

5. The moon is a planet.

Cooling Down

Are the following statements right or wrong?

1. Audrey Hepburn received an Oscar posthumously.

2. La Paz is the capital of Peru.

3. Sushi is a Japanese meal.

4. Squirrels are mammals.

5. Wounded Knee happened in 1900.

No Pain, No _____

Can you supply the beginning words of each of the following proverbs?

1. _____ killed the cat.

2. _____ the doctor away.

3. _____ by ear.

No Pain, No _____

Can you supply the beginning words of each of the following proverbs?

1. _____ its weakest link.

2. _____ are soon parted.

3. _____ and hear no lies.

No Pain, No _____

Can you supply the beginning words of each of the following proverbs?

1. _____ only skin deep.

2. _____ can't be choosers.

3. _____ cats and dogs.

No Pain, No _____

Can you supply the beginning words of each of the following proverbs?

1. _____ before they are hatched.

2. _____ what you sow.

3. _____ with fire.

Medium
Puzzles

No Pain, No _____

Can you supply the beginning words of each of the following proverbs?

1. _____ catches the worm.

2. _____ number one.

3. _____ a bowl of cherries.

No Pain, No _____

Can you supply the beginning words of each of the following proverbs?

1. _____ divided we fall.

2. _____ spoil the broth.

3. _____ justifies the means.

Entangled Figures

Examine the image below; then determine which three of the nine figures below it are combined to form the image.

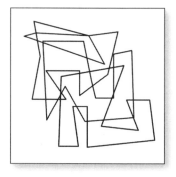

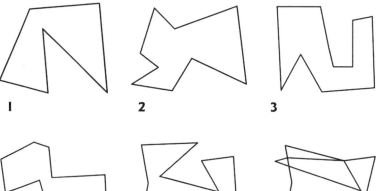

1

2

3

4

5

6

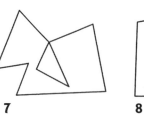

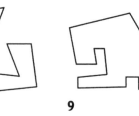

7

8

9

Entangled Figures

Examine the image below; then determine which three of the nine figures below it are combined to form the image.

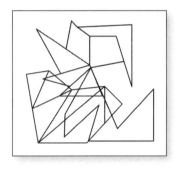

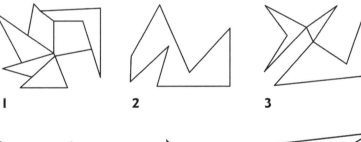

1

2

3

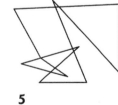

4

5

6

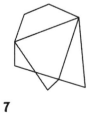

7

8

9

Entangled Figures

Examine the image below; then determine which three of the nine figures below it are combined to form the image.

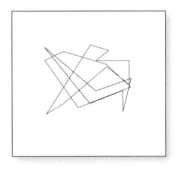

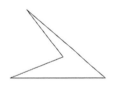

1

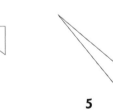

2

3

4

5

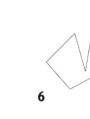

6

7

8

9

Entangled Figures

Examine the image below; then determine which three of the nine figures below it are combined to form the image.

1

2

3

4

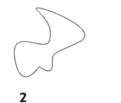

5

6

7

8

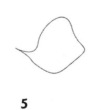

9

Towers of Hanoi

Determine the fewest number of moves necessary to change the configuration in Figure A to that shown in Figure B. You may not place a larger disk on a smaller one, and you may move only one disk at a time.

A

B

Towers of Hanoi

Determine the fewest number of moves necessary to change the configuration in Figure A to that shown in Figure B. You may not place a larger disk on a smaller one, and you may move only one disk at a time.

A

B

Throwing a Curve

Read the following story and pick out the three things that don't quite make sense.

Ms. Cole was driving. She had just dropped her son Rupert in front of his school and was now driving toward her shop. Her car was absolutely packed with cardboard boxes, all the way up to the roof of her car, from the passenger seat all the way to the trunk. Inside the boxes were dozens of artificial plants that one customer had ordered the week before for a wedding. Suddenly, someone honked a horn at her, and she jumped so high that she literally bumped into the roof of her car. She glanced into her rearview mirror and saw two drivers arguing about a parking space. She would have thought traffic was going to be quieter on Christmas day.

Throwing a Curve

Read the following story and pick out the three things that don't quite make sense.

Caroline had been hired in August in the archives department of the public library. She constantly got lost in the five floors of this huge building, patiently strolling along the corridors with her trolley full of books. After one month, the curator permanently assigned her to the fourth floor, which was a great relief to Caroline— she often got lost going from one floor to the other. She was also excited because this top floor of the library contained only the rarest and oldest printed books; some of them were more than seven centuries old! Sometimes she would take a break from work to see her friend in the new books department. She met this friend the very day she was hired, when the two of them had lunch together in a cozy restaurant and passed the time talking about the books they loved while watching the snow fall outside the window.

Easy as One-Two-Three

Take a careful look at the figure below and count the number of triangles it has.

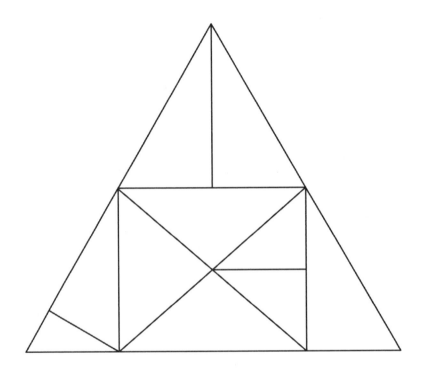

Easy as One-Two-Three

Take a careful look at the figure below and count the number of triangles it has.

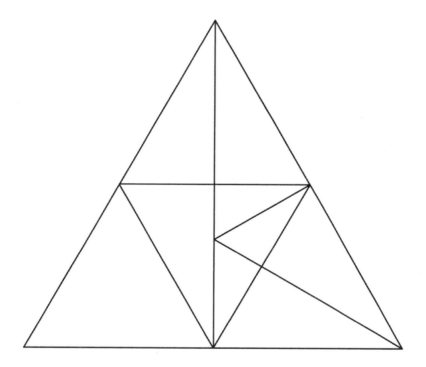

Easy as One-Two-Three

Take a careful look at the figure below and count the number of triangles it has.

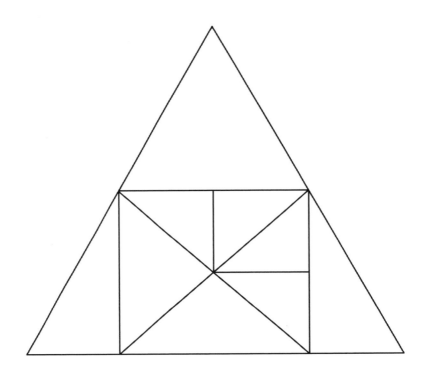

Can You Spot Me?

Find the odd one in this series.

Can You Spot Me?

Find the odd one in this series.

ꝺꝺꝺꝺꝺꝺꝺꝺꝺꝺꝺꝺꝺꝺꝺꝺꝺꝺꝺꝺꝺꝺꝺꝺꝺꝺꝺꝺꝺꝺ

ꝺꝺꝺꝺꝺꝺꝺꝺꝺꝺꝺꝺꝺꝺꝺꝺꝺꝺꝺꝺꝺꝺꝺꝺꝺꝺꝺꝺꝺꝺ

ꝺꝺꝺꝺꝺꝺꝺꝺꝺꝺꝺꝺꝺꝺꝺꝺꝺꝺꝺꝺꝺꝺꝺꝺꝺꝺꝺꝺꝺ

ꝺꝺꝺꝺꝺꝺꝺꝺꝺꝺꝺꝺꝺꝺꝺꝺꝺꝺꝺꝺꝺꝺꝺꝺꝺꝺꝺꝺꝺ

Warming Up

Read the text below and write down all of the "oo" (as in "cool") and "i" (as in "bit") sounds.

She did not really have the choice anyway. The two of them had decided the boy would finish school soon. The fruit of all her efforts could be ruined if the rules were not respected, she thought. What good was there in trying to find him a job if he was going to have his foolish behavior again, as soon as he was out of his room? This solution was as suitable as going out with a flu under pouring rain. She too had her opinion about this, and one that did not need proofing: it came straight from experience. When he grew older, he would understand.

Warming Up

Read the text below and write down all of the "a" (as in "say") and "i" (as in "ice") sounds.

The dentist's face looked tense. The man had tried to make his best, but he clearly needed a break. The heat was great too, and many flies also took a close look at the operation. The price to pay was high, as the horse could die from the surgery, and it was not the kind of horse that one could find every day. This one had won many races, and the day of the Grand National, you could hear people pray, so silent was the audience. The owner, a brave man from Colorado, had chased for years before finding the horse of his life. His wife had left long ago, and all that remained from her now was memories.

Incomplete Workout

Which of the four tiles below completes the picture?

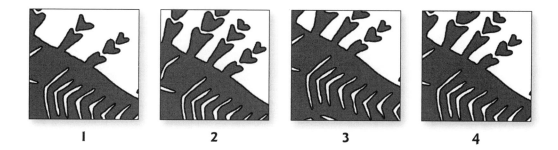

1   2   3   4

Incomplete Workout

Which of the four tiles below completes the picture?

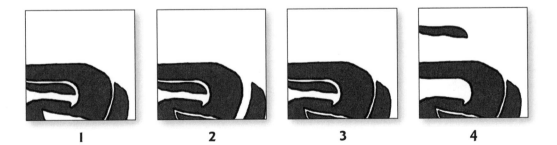

1   2   3   4

Hidden Strength

Find the fifteen words hidden in the grid. They can be read horizontally, vertically, or diagonally; backward or forward; up or down. The same letter can be used in several different words.

HINT: *the theme is* **clothes**.

```
S  D  E  A  V  N  E  J  K  T  K  L
F  M  T  M  S  D  S  G  U  I  H  K
V  N  R  R  U  E  E  H  J  T  H  G
E  W  I  C  O  T  T  O  N  V  G  N
T  G  K  H  W  V  S  E  B  S  Z  O
T  F  S  R  E  S  U  O  R  T  O  L
E  S  N  D  E  N  I  M  C  O  S  Y
P  Z  A  Z  D  F  T  D  A  C  S  N
O  A  F  J  L  Y  B  F  P  K  E  S
L  V  C  H  V  J  H  K  X  I  R  X
O  V  L  A  U  N  D  R  Y  N  D  E
S  C  D  T  N  E  M  R  A  G  N  G
```

Hidden Strength

Find the fifteen words hidden in the grid. They can be read horizontally, vertically, or diagonally; backward or forward; up or down. The same letter can be used in several different words.

HINT: *the theme is* **family**.

F	G	B	J	R	A	R	E	Y	U	K	V
A	F	S	F	R	Y	M	M	O	M	Y	I
Q	N	A	A	D	O	P	T	I	O	N	F
H	E	J	D	C	C	T	C	Z	B	Z	H
Z	R	N	N	K	I	N	S	H	I	P	E
F	D	S	O	R	I	E	H	H	R	A	R
D	L	S	E	S	Z	R	J	E	T	P	E
S	I	B	U	N	Z	A	J	Z	H	A	H
D	H	O	H	F	E	P	D	V	K	R	T
A	C	C	D	A	U	G	H	T	E	R	A
D	Y	T	S	A	N	Y	D	L	T	P	F
O	I	D	Y	G	O	L	A	E	N	E	G

Working Both Sides

Take a careful look at these two sets of characters. Which characters appear in the series on the right but not in the series on the left?

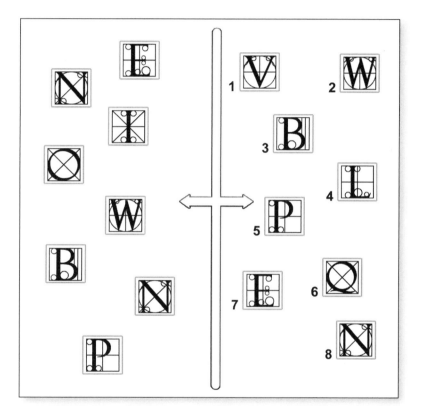

Working Both Sides

Take a careful look at these two sets of characters. Which characters appear in the series on the right but not in the series on the left?

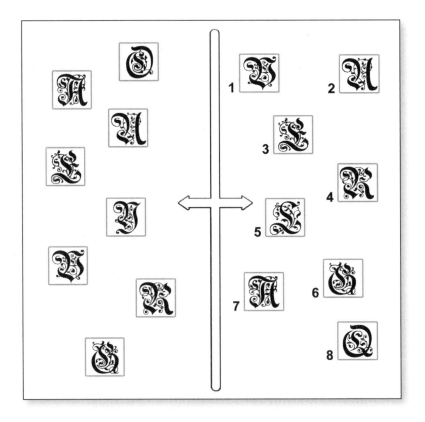

The Circuit Workout

Try to find the logical order of the pictures below.

It Takes Two

Which two dragons are exactly alike?

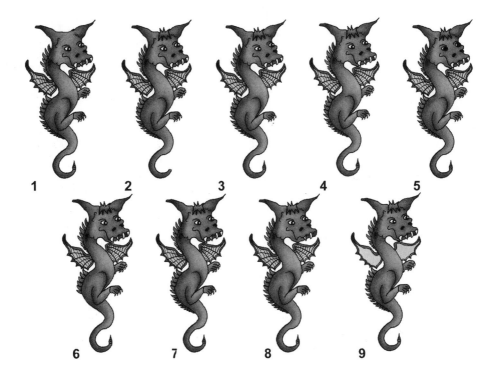

It Takes Two

Which two policemen are exactly alike?

Pencils Up

Link the ten rhombuses without raising your pencil. You cannot touch the other figures, and you cannot go between two figures more than once.

Pencils Up

Link the ten stars with eight branches without raising your pencil. You cannot touch the other figures, and you cannot go between two figures more than once.

Power Squats

Find a seven-letter word in the grid below. The first two letters are shown in the shaded squares. Letters must be adjacent to the next letter in the word.

G	T	I	P
U	I	H	J
R	T	S	A
E	**Y**	E	L

Power Squats

Find an eight-letter word in the grid below. The first two letters
are shown in the shaded squares. Letters must be adjacent to the next
letter in the word.

E	Y	T	I
R	L	U	R
Y	M	C	**E**
C	I	B	**S**

Power Squats

Find an eight-letter word in the grid below. The first two letters are shown in the shaded squares. Letters must be adjacent to the next letter in the word.

R	E	T	B
S	S	N	L
D	**R**	I	O
E	**P**	T	U

Power Squats

Find a seven-letter word in the grid below. The first two letters are shown in the shaded squares. Letters must be adjacent to the next letter in the word.

A	**R**	R	I
N	C	A	V
G	Y	L	V
O	N	E	E

Solo or Group Exercise?

This grid contains four singular nouns and four plural nouns. Can you find them?

criterion   sock   glasses   children

nail   box   stairs   foxes

In this grid, classify the nouns as singular or plural, and write them down in alphabetical order.

Singular	Plural

Solo or Group Exercise?

This grid contains four singular nouns and four plural nouns. Can you find them?

geese	shoe	feet	women
hemisphere	cheese	tribe	sketches

In this grid, classify the nouns as singular or plural, and write them down in alphabetical order.

Singular	Plural

Solo or Group Exercise?

This grid contains four singular nouns and four plural nouns. Can you find them?

people	bear	eyelash	teeth
sins	crane	halves	silver

In this grid, classify the nouns as singular or plural, and write them down in alphabetical order.

Singular	Plural

Solo or Group Exercise?

This grid contains four singular nouns and four plural nouns. Can you find them?

mouse	supplies	mice	city
speed	prices	excess	thieves

In this grid, classify the nouns as singular or plural, and write them down in alphabetical order.

Singular	Plural

Conditioning

Classify the ten items in this list in two categories, and title each category.

Thai-boxing	aïkido
volleyball	judo
handball	soccer
karate	rugby
tae kwon do	basketball

Title:	Title:

Conditioning

Classify the ten items in this list in two categories, and title each category.

snowboarding	bobsledding
water-skiing	skiing
mountaineering	ice hockey
wakeboarding	surfing
sailing	windsurfing

Title: _____   **Title:** _____

Conditioning

Classify the ten items in this list in two categories, and title each category.

Henry James	Texas
The Rolling Stones	John Irving
Black Eyed Peas	Nathaniel Hawthorne
Pink Floyd	Francis Scott Fitzgerald
James Joyce	The Doors

Title: _____ **Title:** _____

Conditioning

Classify the ten items in this list in two categories, and title each category.

Mozart	Schubert
Andy Warhol	Debussy
Berlioz	J. M. Basquiat
Leonardo Da Vinci	Chopin
Lucian Freud	Salvador Dali

Title: _____ **Title:** _____

Alignment

Find the word that corresponds to the definition.

1. straight line segment that passes through the center and whose endpoints are on the circular boundary

    diameter   radius   perimeter

2. food made from flour, water, and sometimes eggs, which is mixed, kneaded and formed into various shapes, and boiled prior to consumption

    doughnut   pasta   cake

Alignment

Find the word that corresponds to the definition.

1. succession of rulers who are members of the same family for generations

   decade   **dynasty**   **genealogy**

2. writing individual instrument that applies ink to some surface, mostly paper

   pen   **keyboard**   **screen**

Alignment

Find the word that corresponds to the definition.

1. view of an object or scene consisting of the outline and a featureless interior

   shadow   **silhouette**   **profile**

2. Japanese word for comics and/or cartoons

   manga   **kimono**   **sari**

Alignment

Find the word that corresponds to the definition.

1. barrier across flowing water that obstructs, directs, or retards the flow, often creating a reservoir, lake, or impoundment

   bridge　　　**dam**　　　**viaduct**

2. board game and mental-skill game for two players, played on a square board of eight rows and eight columns

   checkers　　　**dice**　　　**chess**

Alignment

Find the word that corresponds to the definition.

1. medical disorder characterized by varying or persistent elevated blood sugar levels, especially after eating

   cancer   **illness**   **diabetes**

2. small mammals sometimes affectionately known as bunnies

   mice   **rabbits**   **dogs**

Lateral Raises

The letters of the following words have been mixed up. They are all related to movies. The first letter of each word is given as a clue.

OOSTIGNH: S_____

MEACAR: C_____

CASTSRE: A_____

SITGNAC: C_____

Lateral Raises

The letters of the following words have been mixed up. They are all related to movies. The first letter of each word is given as a clue.

MTOINAANI: A＿＿＿＿＿＿＿＿＿＿＿＿＿＿＿

TTLSBUISE: S＿＿＿＿＿＿＿＿＿＿＿＿＿＿＿

OGLAIDUE: D＿＿＿＿＿＿＿＿＿＿＿＿＿＿

OIRANESC: S＿＿＿＿＿＿＿＿＿＿＿＿＿＿

Lateral Raises

The letters of the following words have been mixed up. They are all related to movies or weather. The first letter of each word is given as a clue.

TROIDCRE: D_____

KCARUONSDT: S_____

REOFACST: F_____

MUTREAREEPT: T_____

Lateral Raises

The letters of the following words have been mixed up. They are all related to weather. The first letter of each word is given as a clue.

AFHERNHTIE: F_____

MSOPEAHRET: A_____

IAELCMT: C_____

HGTUISNL: S_____

Lateral Raises

The letters of the following words have been mixed up. They are all related to weather. The first letter of each word is given as a clue.

ODTROAN: T_____

RRUHIANCE: H_____

TSEEITLAL: S_____

RTROABMEE: B_____

Basketball in New York

Determine the minimum number of moves needed to move from the configuration in Figure A to the configuration in Figure B. Follow these rules:

- Balls may move out of baskets only upward.
- You may not place more than three balls in one basket.
- You may move only one ball at a time.

A

B

Basketball in New York

Determine the minimum number of moves needed to move from the configuration in Figure A to the configuration in Figure B. Follow these rules:

- Balls may move out of baskets only upward.
- You may not place more than three balls in one basket.
- You may move only one ball at a time.

A

B

No Problem!

Solve this mathematical problem in your head.

To create suits for a drama, a seamstress buys:
- 25 thread spools of 10 feet each,
- 30 ribbons of 100 inches each,
- 7 wool balls of 7 feet each

What is the total length of these elements?

No Problem!

Solve this mathematical problem in your head.

The size of a particular algae doubles every day. Knowing it will take
forty days for the algae to cover the surface of a pool, how many days will it need
to cover one-quarter of the pool?

No Problem!

Solve this mathematical problem in your head.

Miss Smith would like to buy a car. The first car seller she meets shows her a $25,000 model and offers Miss Smith a 5 percent discount if she buys the car immediately. Another car seller shows her a $22,000 model with a 4 percent discount only.

1. Which deal offers the bigger discount?

_____

2. With the discount, which vehicle is less expensive?

_____

No Problem!

Solve this mathematical problem in your head.

Mr. Martin counts his jam jars. All the jars except three contain apricots; all the jars except three contain prunes; all the jars except three contain raspberries; all the jars except three contain cherries.

How many jam jars does Mr. Martin have?

No Mistakes Allowed

Find the correct spelling of each word among the three options.

constitutional	constitussionnal	constitutionnal
harmonie	harmmony	harmony
comedie	comedy	commedy
millionnaire	millonaire	millionaire

No Mistakes Allowed

Find the correct spelling of each word among the three options.

obsolete	obsolette	obsolite
armamment	armament	armmement
literaly	literrally	literally
multiplicity	multiplisity	multipplicity

No Mistakes Allowed

Find the correct spelling of each word among the three options.

curently	currently	currentlly
elephant	ellephant	elefant
sustainnability	sustainabillity	sustainability
cowardisse	cowardice	kowardice

No Mistakes Allowed

Find the correct spelling of each word among the three options.

athmosphere	atemosphere	atmosphere
furniture	ferniture	furnitture
stroberry	strawberry	strawbery
impresive	impressive	imppressive

No Mistakes Allowed

Find the correct spelling of each word among the three options.

loyallty	loyaltty	loyalty
exppression	expresion	expression
parallel	paralel	parrallel
medecine	medicine	midicine

No Mistakes Allowed

Find the correct spelling of each word among the three options.

disagreement	disagrement	disagreemment
humilliation	humiliation	hummiliation
powerfully	powerfuly	powerffully
orchestra	orrchestra	orkestra

Spinning Class

Determine which figure is a mirror image of the others

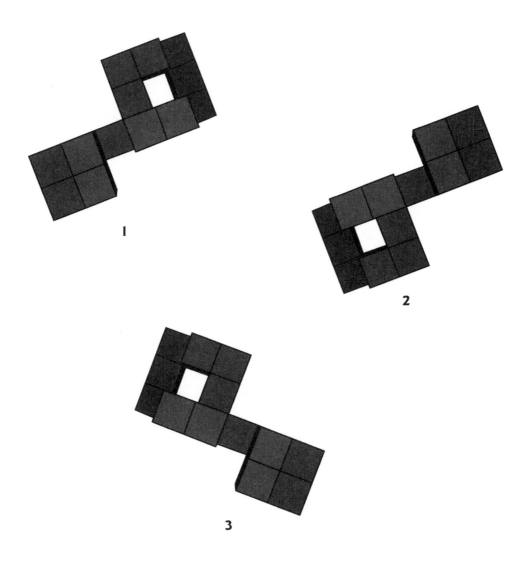

1

2

3

Spinning Class

Determine which figure is a mirror image of the others

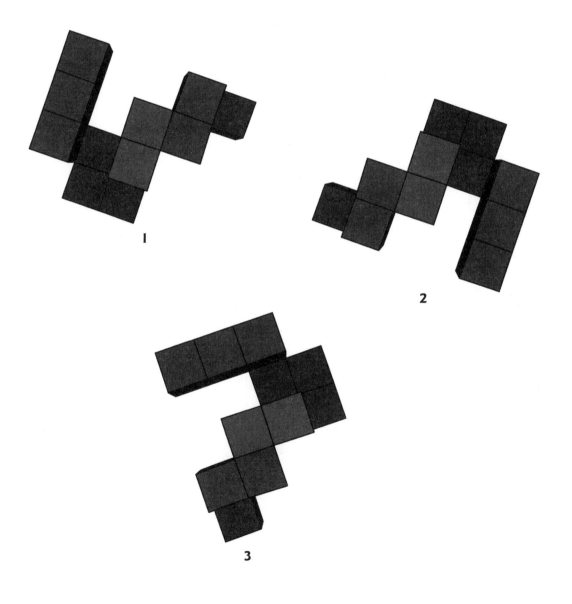

1

2

3

Muscle Memory

Match each author with the book that he or she wrote.

1. Herman Melville   **A.** *The Age of Innocence*

2. Mark Twain   **B.** *Huckleberry Finn*

3. Jack London   **C.** *Dubliners*

4. Edith Wharton   **D.** *Moby-Dick*

5. James Joyce   **E.** *White Fang*

Muscle Memory

Match each tint with its closest basic color.

1. lavender   **A.** brown

2. turquoise   **B.** purple

3. cream   **C.** blue

4. gold   **D.** white

5. chocolate   **E.** yellow

Muscle Memory

Match each dish with its country or area of origin.

1. tandoori chicken   **A.** Italy

2. spring rolls   **B.** Mexico

3. chili con carne   **C.** India

4. couscous   **D.** China

5. spaghetti Bolognese   **E.** North Africa

Muscle Memory

Match each physician specialist with his or her specialty.

1. ophtalmologist   **A.** skin

2. dermatologist   **B.** children

3. oncologist   **C.** mental diseases

4. pediatrician   **D.** eyes

5. psychiatrist   **E.** cancer

Muscle Memory

Match each bone with its location in the human body.

1. femur		**A.** thigh	
2. parietal		**B.** shin	
3. clavicle		**C.** skull	
4. tibia		**D.** back	
5. vertebra		**E.** shoulder	

Muscle Memory

Match each plant with the plant group to which it belongs.

1. amanita   **A.** mushroom

2. poplar   **B.** cereal

3. fucus   **C.** tree

4. corn   **D.** herb

5. oregano   **E.** alga

Muscle Memory

Match each U.S. president with the year in which he was elected.

1. Franklin Delano Roosevelt   **A.** 1961

2. Theodore Roosevelt   **B.** 1933

3. Richard Nixon   **C.** 1981

4. John F. Kennedy   **D.** 1901

5. Ronald Reagan   **E.** 1969

Muscle Memory

Match each unit of measurement with what it measures.

1. hertz　　　　　　**A.** length

2. league　　　　　**B.** frequency

3. ton　　　　　　　**C.** time

4. hectare　　　　　**D.** weight

5. minute　　　　　**E.** surface

Working Both Sides

Take a careful look at these two sets of characters. Which characters appear in the series on the right but not in the series on the left?

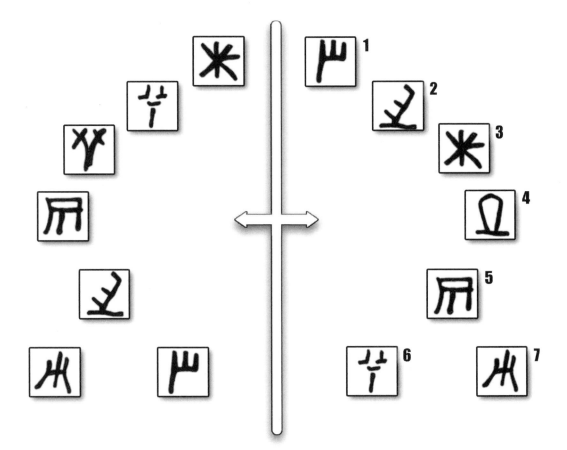

Working Both Sides

Take a careful look at these two sets of characters. Which characters appear in the series on the right but not in the series on the left?

Interval Training

Can you put back together the ten three-part words that have been split and spread across the grid? Each part can be used only once, and the splits may not necessarily be the part splits you find in the dictionary.

HINT: *The theme is* **emotions and feelings.**

mo	ve	a	ry	des
ge	tion	jea	ffec	sy
plea	eu	si	ra	re
ria	bra	lou	ty	duc
cou	su	de	tien	pho
se	re	ce	pa	tion

1. _____

2. _____

3. _____

4. _____

5. _____

6. _____

7. _____

8. _____

9. _____

10. _____

Interval Training

Can you put back together the ten three-part words that have been split and spread across the grid? Each part can be used only once, and the splits may not necessarily be the part splits you find in the dictionary.

HINT: *The theme is* **emotions and feelings.**

a	se	tion	pri	tion
ha	out	dread	tas	ppi
te	der	ge	sen	ness
sur	ment	sa	ra	se
ful	ness	sen	fflic	ti
ry	ten	dis	ness	mi

1. _____   6. _____

2. _____   7. _____

3. _____   8. _____

4. _____   9. _____

5. _____   10. _____

Interval Training

Can you put back together the ten three-part words that have been split and spread across the grid? Each part can be used only once, and the splits may not necessarily be the part splits you find in the dictionary.

HINT: *The theme is* **animals.**

ri	tu	cka	ri	phant
e	ffe	go	mos	li
na	lla	too	ra	roo
can	vul	le	ca	to
ca	co	ga	pe	bou
kan	ry	gi	qui	re

1. _____

2. _____

3. _____

4. _____

5. _____

6. _____

7. _____

8. _____

9. _____

10. _____

Interval Training

Can you put back together the ten three-part words that have been split and spread across the grid? Each part can be used only once, and the splits may not necessarily be the part splits you find in the dictionary.

HINT: *The theme is* **animals.**

go	pan	ea	e	co
lo	ve	cro	bird	zee
a	ant	to	min	la
fla	hy	bu	o	ter
pard	ko	dile	lo	pus
oc	le	chim	na	ffa

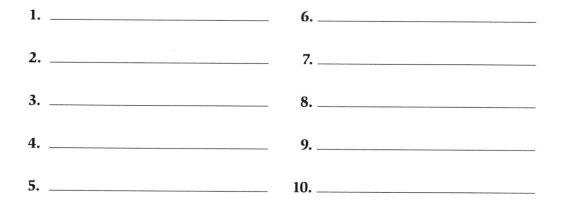

1. _____   6. _____

2. _____   7. _____

3. _____   8. _____

4. _____   9. _____

5. _____   10. _____

Combination Sets

Take a careful look at the six elements below and try to determine which ones are not part of the larger figure. Beware, some elements may just have been turned around.

1   2   3

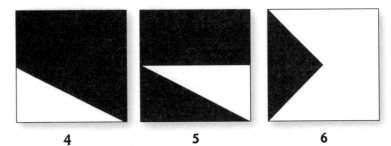

4   5   6

Combination Sets

Take a careful look at the six elements below and try to determine which ones are not part of the larger figure. Beware, some elements may just have been turned around.

Distance Run

Take a careful look at the location of the seven objects in this landscape.

The image below shows the same landscape as seen from above. Determine where you would stand in the scenery to view the landscape as it appears in the image above.

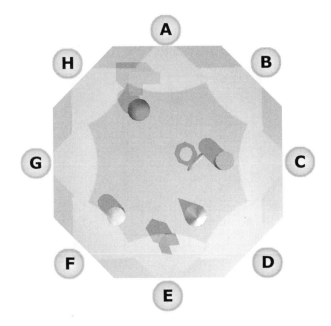

Distance Run

Take a careful look at the location of the seven objects in this landscape.

The image below shows the same landscape as seen from above. Determine where you would stand in the scenery to view the landscape as it appears in the image above.

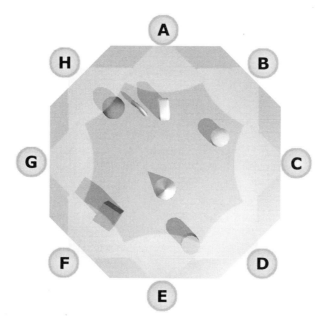

Cross Training

Decipher this quotation about life from Frank Lloyd Wright. Each symbol represents a letter, but it is always the same letter.

Cross Training

Decipher this quotation about dust from D. H. Lawrence. Each symbol represents a letter, but it is always the same letter.

Cross Training

Decipher this quotation about excess from Oscar Wilde. Each symbol represents a letter, but it is always the same letter.

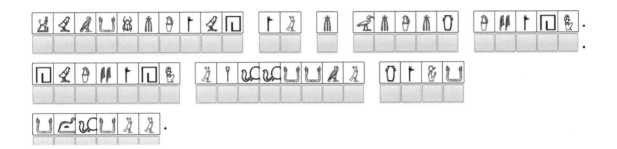

Cross Training

Decipher this quotation about being rude from Rita Mae Brown. Each symbol represents a letter, but it is always the same letter.

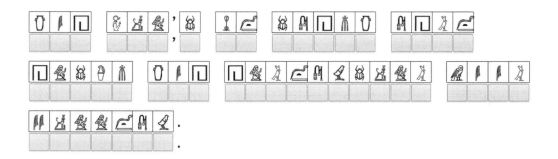

Working the Memory Muscle

Take a minute to memorize the eight words below without looking at the bottom half of the page.

automobile	jam
boat	parasol
information	marriage
bear	cocoa

Now cover up the list of words and answer the following questions:

1. Which word on the list has no plural form?

_____

2. How many abstract words are there on the list? What are they?

_____

3. Which words on the list can be both a noun and a verb?

_____

4. Which words on the list are edible?

_____

Working the Memory Muscle

Take a minute to memorize the eight words below without looking at the bottom half of the page.

jersey	particularity
brown	vanity
apple pie	purple
spinach	hurry

Now cover up the list of words and answer the following questions:

1. Are any colors on the list? If so, which?

_____

2. Are there any fruit names on the list? If so, which?

_____

3. What, if any, abstract words are on the list?

_____

4. Which word is also the name of a state?

_____

Can You Spot Me?

Find the odd one in this series.

HINT: *The odd one is* 🐷.

Can You Spot Me?

Find the odd one in this series.

HINT: *The odd one is* 🐀.

Can You Spot Me?

Find the odd one in this series.

⫷⫷⫷⫷⫷⫷⫷⫷⫷⫷⫷⫷⫷⫷⫷⫷⫷⫷⫷⫷⫷⫷⫷⫷⫷⫷⫷⫷⫷⫷⫷⫷⫷⫷⫷⫷⫷
⫷⫷⫷⫷⫷⫷⫷⫷⫷⫷⫷⫷⫷⫷⫷⫷⫷⫷⫷⫷⫷⫷⫷⫷⫷⫷⫷⫷⫷⫷⫷⫷⫷⫷⫷⫷⫷
⫷⫷⫷⫷⫷⫷⫷⫷⫷⫷⫷⫷⫷⫷⫷⫷⫷⫷⫷⫷⫷⫷⫷⫷⫷⫷⫷⫷⫷⫷⫷⫷⫷⫷⫷⫷⫷
⫷⫷⫷⫷ ⫷ ⫷⫷⫷⫷⫷⫷⫷⫷⫷⫷⫷⫷⫷⫷⫷⫷⫷⫷⫷⫷⫷⫷⫷⫷⫷⫷⫷⫷⫷⫷⫷
⫷⫷⫷⫷⫷⫷⫷⫷⫷⫷⫷⫷⫷⫷⫷⫷⫷⫷⫷⫷⫷⫷⫷⫷⫷⫷⫷⫷⫷⫷⫷⫷⫷⫷⫷⫷⫷
⫷⫷⫷⫷⫷⫷⫷⫷⫷⫷⫷⫷⫷⫷⫷⫷⫷⫷⫷⫷⫷⫷⫷⫷⫷⫷⫷⫷⫷⫷⫷⫷⫷⫷⫷⫷⫷

HINT: *The odd one is* ⫸.

Can You Spot Me?

Find the odd one in this series.

⊘⊘
⊘⊘
⊘⊘
⊘⊘⊘⊘⊘⊘⊘⊘⊘⊘⊘⊘⊘⊘⊘⊘⊘⊘⊘⊘⊘⊘⊘⊘⊘⊘⊘⊘⊘⊘⊘⊘⊘⊘⊘⊘⊝⊘⊘
⊘⊘
⊘⊘

HINT: *The odd one is ⊝.*

Can You Spot Me?

Find the odd one in this series.

☹☹☹☹☹☹☹☹☹☹☹☹☹☹☹☹☹☹☹☹☹☹☹☹☹☹☹☹☹☹☹☹☹☹☹☹
☹☹☹☹☹☹☹☹☹☹☹☹☹☹☹☹☹☹☹☹☹☹☹☹☹☹☹☹☹☹☹☹☹☹☹☹
☹☹☹☹☹☹☹☹☹☹☹☹☹☹☹☹☹☹☹☹☹☹☹☹☹☹☹☹☹☹☹☹☹☹☹☹
☹☹☹☹☹☹☹☹☹☹☹☹☹☹☹☹☹☹☹☹☹☹☹☹☹☹☹☹☹☹☹☹☹☹☹☹
☹☹☹☹☹☹☹☹☹☹☹☹☹☹☹☹☹☹☹☹☹☹☹☹☹☹☹☹☹☹☹☹☹☹☹☹
☹☹☹☹☹☹☹☹☹☹☹☹☹☹☹☹☹☹☹☹☹☹☹☹☹☹☹☹☹☹☹☹☹☹☹☹

HINT: *The odd one is ☺.*

Can You Spot Me?

Find the odd one in this series.

HINT: *The odd one is 🗎.*

Can You Spot Me?

Find the odd one in this series.

ଷ୍ୱ ଷ୍ୱ
ଷ୍ୱ ⮞ ଷ୍ୱ
ଷ୍ୱ ଷ୍ୱ
ଷ୍ୱ ଷ୍ୱ
ଷ୍ୱ ଷ୍ୱ
ଷ୍ୱ ଷ୍ୱ

HINT: *The odd one is* ⮞ *.*

Can You Spot Me?

Find the odd one in this series.

HINT: *The odd one is* ⏻.

No Pain, No _____

Can you supply the beginning words of each of the following proverbs?

1. _____ than never.

2. _____ is bliss.

3. _____ reckoned with.

No Pain, No _____

Can you supply the beginning words of each of the following proverbs?

1. _____ grow fonder.

2. _____ with pleasure.

3. _____ and go.

No Pain, No _____

Can you supply the beginning words of each of the following proverbs?

1. _____ the best medicine.

2. _____ to pay Paul.

3. _____ goes unpunished.

No Pain, No _____

Can you supply the beginning words of each of the following proverbs?

1. _____ and eat it too.

2. _____ say never.

3. _____ deserves another.

Hard
Puzzles

No Pain, No _____

Can you supply the beginning words of each of the following proverbs?

1. _____ easy go.

2. _____ of my enemy is my friend.

3. _____ make good neighbors.

No Pain, No _____

Can you supply the beginning words of each of the following proverbs?

1. _____ in one basket.

2. _____ for the trees.

3. _____ to spite your face.

Entangled Figures

Examine the image below; then determine which three of the nine figures below it are combined to form the image.

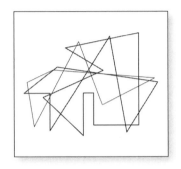

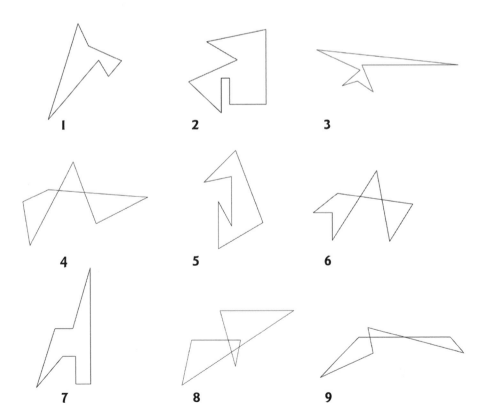

1

2

3

4

5

6

7

8

9

All-Star Game

Of the nine words below, only six can be placed in the star. Arrows indicate the direction in which each word is placed.

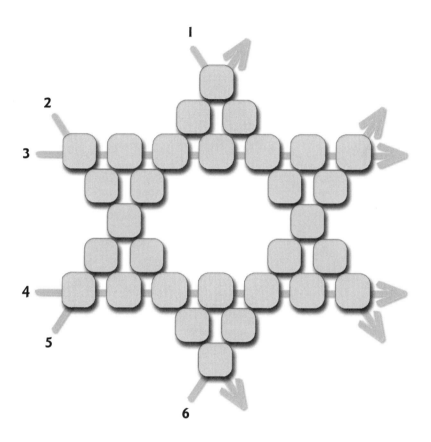

TYPHOON

FREEZER

SOLVENT

EPISODE

PORTION

STATION

TRILOGY

STEEPLE

SULFATE

All-Star Game

Of the nine words below, only six can be placed in the star. Arrows indicate the direction in which each word is placed.

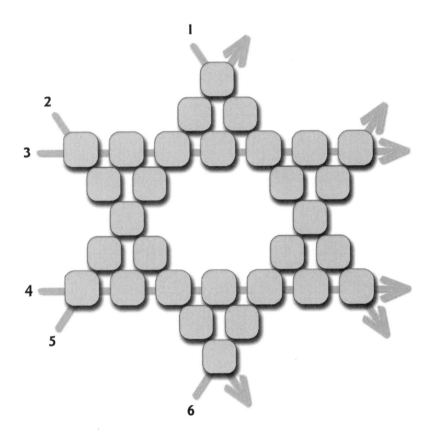

HARDTOP	HOSPICE
BRIGADE	BREADTH
BIBELOT	MODESTY
GRAVITY	MEETING
DISGUST	

All-Star Game

Of the nine words below, only six can be placed in the star. Arrows indicate the direction in which each word is placed.

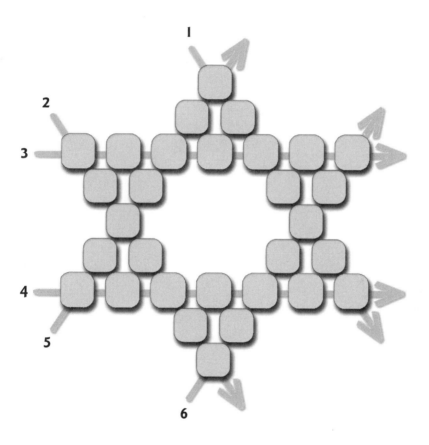

CARBINE	VERDICT
AVARICE	ARSENIC
DENDRON	EDITION
DISEASE	NITRATE
COOKING	

All-Star Game

Of the nine words below, only six can be placed in the star. Arrows indicate the direction in which each word is placed.

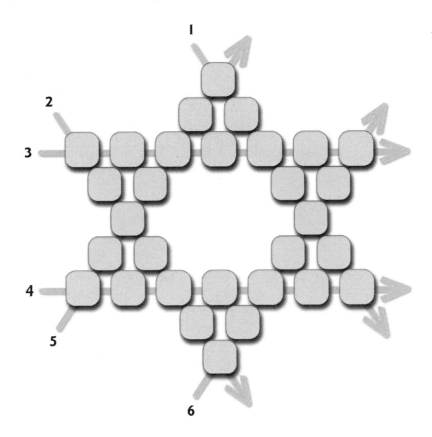

GRAVITY

SURFING

SUICIDE

MASSAGE

GELATIN

SALSIFY

SOILAGE

SURPLUS

PRELATE

Towers of Hanoi

Determine the fewest number of moves necessary to change the configuration in Figure A to that shown in Figure B. You may not place a larger disk on a smaller one, and you may move only one disk at a time.

A

B

Towers of Hanoi

Determine the fewest number of moves necessary to change the configuration in Figure A to that shown in Figure B. You may not place a larger disk on a smaller one, and you may move only one disk at a time.

A

B

Towers of Hanoi

Determine the fewest number of moves necessary to change the configuration in Figure A to that shown in Figure B. You may not place a larger disk on a smaller one, and you may move only one disk at a time.

A

B

Easy as One-Two-Three

Take a careful look at the figure below and count the number of squares and triangles it has.

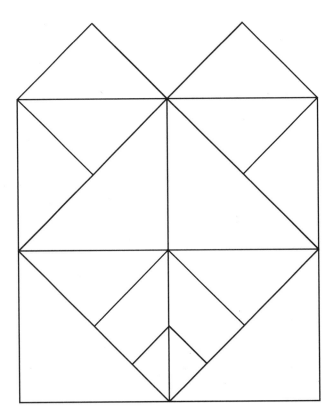

Easy as One-Two-Three

Take a careful look at the figure below and count the number of squares and triangles it has.

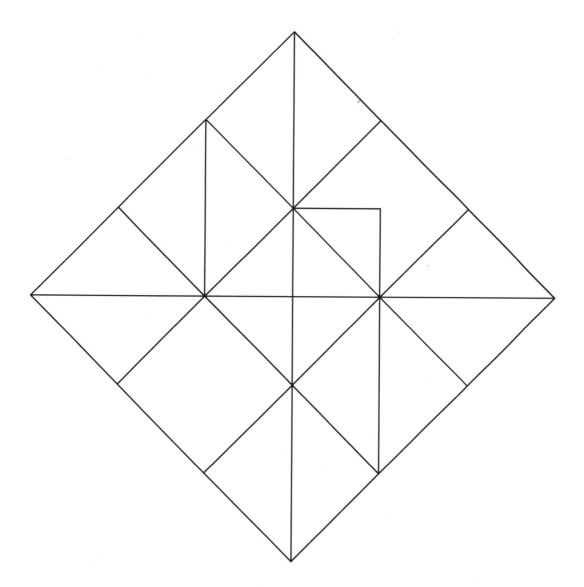

Throwing a Curve

Read the following story and pick out the four things that don't quite make sense.

This morning Jane had difficulty getting her young horse out of its stable. She tried to talk to him softly and persuade him to get out but nothing worked, and the beautiful Friesian would not budge. The caretaker was a bit worried because the race was to happen the next day, April 31, and the horse was showing signs of not wanting to run. It was necessary to train today, especially since tomorrow's race would probably be the last before its retirement from competition. When the horse finally decided to walk out on the leaf-covered ground, he looked sad and depressed, and Jane finally noticed that one of his legs looked sore and that he limped a bit. She called the vet immediately. He reassured her, telling her it was nothing serious.

Throwing a Curve

Read the following story and pick out the four things that don't quite make sense.

After the six-hour flight from Dallas, Mary and Dave finally landed in Sydney for their three-week honeymoon, anxious to embark on the vacation of their dreams. After leaving the luggage at the hotel, the young Texan couple decided to take a tour on an open-top bus to get a first glimpse of the city. And they became enchanted by it. Hand in hand, they wandered carelessly for hours in the lively streets, without feeling any fatigue from the jet lag. After a few days more in Sydney, they ventured inland, where they met incredible people and even more incredible animals. Dave, a fan of reptiles, was completely awed by all the strange and wonderful creatures they encountered, while his fiancée was much more taken with the kangaroos, koalas, and pandas they saw. One week later, when they were showing their pictures to their friends back in Texas, they were astonished to learn that they had shot more than a thousand photographs! They gave the address of their travel agent to whomever wanted it, because they had such a wonderful time in the land down under.

Can You Spot Me?

Find the odd one in this series.

%*<&~#{[| |`\^@@]})=″#&^)=]}<&~#{[ | |`\^@@]})=}{{@*″#&^)]}}{<&~#{[| |`\^@@]}
)={[<(_@)=]}}{{*″#)=]}}{{&^)<-)=°+*&~@)=]}}{{*″#&^)<#{[| |`\^@@]})=~!§>&″(_-
)=°+*/-+.§!!!§://,<&~#{[| |`@)=]}}{{*″#&^)<@)=]}}{{*″#&^)<\^@@]})=]}}{{[~!§(_-
)=°+*>&/,<&~#{[| |`\^@)=]}}{{*″#&^)<&~#{[ | |`@)=,<&~#{[| |`@)=]}}]}}{{*″#&^)<@)
=]}}{{*″#&^)?<\^@@]})=&~#{[| |`\,<&~#{[ | |`@)=]}}^@@]})=″#&^)=]}<&~#{[| |`\^@
@]})=}{{@*″#&^)]}}{<&~#{[| |`\^@@]})={[<(_@),<&~#{[ | |`@)=]}}@)=]}}]}}{{*″#&^))

HINT: *The odd one is* ?.

Can You Spot Me?

Find the odd one in this series.

HINT: *The odd one is ꜱ.*

Can You Spot Me?

Find the odd one in this series.

♈ ♉ ♌ ♍ ♂ ♋ ♍ ♌ ☊ ♋ ♎ ♊ ☋ ♉ ♈ ♍ ♌ ☋ ♋ ♌ ♍ ☊ ♏ ♍ ♎ ♈ ♊
♑ ♍ ♂ ♋ ♈ ♍ ♌ ♏ ♋ ♍ ♐ ♋ ♌ ♎ ♋ ☋ ♏ ☊ ♋ ☋ ♋ ♍ ♋ ♌
♌ ♋ ☋ ♏ ♏ ♋ ♍ ♋ ♍ ☊ ♑ ♏ ♋ ♌ ♋ ♈ ♍ ♂ ♊ ☊ ♍ ♂ ♏ ♌ ♋ ♊ ☋
♋ ☊ ♋ ♌ ☊ ♋ ♌ ♋ ♌ ♍ ♂ ♏ ♌ ♍ ♂ ♏ ♌ ♋ ♈ ♍ ♂ ♊ ☋ ♋ ♈ ♋
♏ ☋ ♋ ♋ ♍ ♂ ♊ ♍ ♋ ♑ ♌ ♏ ♏ ♋ ☋ ♍ ♋ ♍ ♌ ♏ ♏ ♍ ♂ ♏ ♊ ♏ ♍
♂ ♏ ♌ ♋ ♋ ♌ ♏ ♋ ♏ ♒ ♊ ♈ ♈ ♒ ☊ ♋ ♋ ♏ ♒ ♓ ♏ ♋ ♋ ♋ ✗ ✓ ☊ ♋ ♍ ♂ ♏ ♌

HINT: *The odd one is ♏.*

Incomplete Workout

Which of the five tiles below complete the picture?

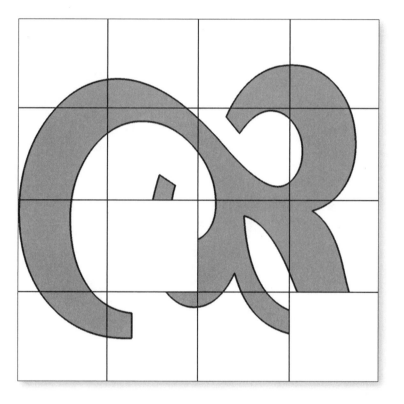

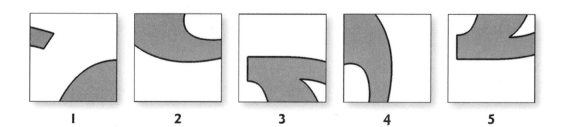

1   2   3   4   5

Incomplete Workout

Which of the five tiles below complete the picture?

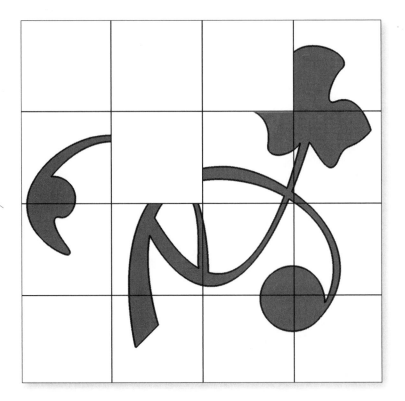

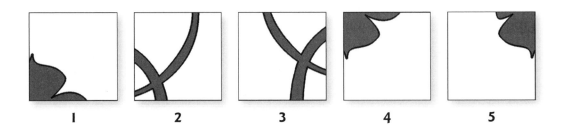

1   2   3   4   5

Hidden Strength

Find the twenty words hidden in the grid. They can be read horizontally, vertically, or diagonally; backward or forward; up or down. The same letter can be used in several different words.

HINT: *the theme is* **animals**.

```
S  D  F  G  H  T  A  F  V  A  E  C
W  X  R  K  R  C  H  O  O  F  E  D
G  H  G  H  S  E  I  C  E  P  S  F
H  Z  N  Y  I  S  F  E  K  R  D  Y
T  N  I  P  A  N  T  M  U  E  Z  G
O  D  L  P  E  I  O  F  X  F  J  O
L  D  R  U  F  N  C  A  L  F  Z  L
S  B  A  P  K  V  C  B  E  A  R  O
B  R  E  E  D  I  N  G  P  R  C  O
C  F  Y  E  N  O  X  A  K  I  O  Z
W  O  L  F  I  B  W  S  S  G  V  S
X  V  E  L  A  M  M  A  M  D  M  E
```

Hidden Strength

Find the twenty words hidden in the grid. They can be read horizontally, vertically, or diagonally; backward or forward; up or down. The same letter can be used in several different words.

HINT: *the theme is* **plants and botanicals**.

```
T  R  E  E  G  A  R  D  E  N  N  M
A  F  C  Z  G  E  Z  P  A  R  K  O
J  T  R  V  J  T  D  O  G  E  I  S
F  R  E  V  R  G  E  R  L  F  D  S
N  U  E  N  I  E  E  C  A  X  U  W
E  N  W  W  B  P  S  E  K  G  J  N
H  K  T  I  O  N  L  U  N  V  F  R
C  T  D  L  K  L  D  U  N  G  D  W
I  F  L  L  A  O  F  H  E  D  E  B
L  E  E  O  O  H  B  C  E  Z  E  V
N  G  R  W  G  E  H  E  F  E  W  W
H  O  R  T  I  C  U  L  T  U  R  E
```

Working Both Sides

Take a careful look at these two sets of characters. Which characters appear in the series on the right but not in the series on the left?

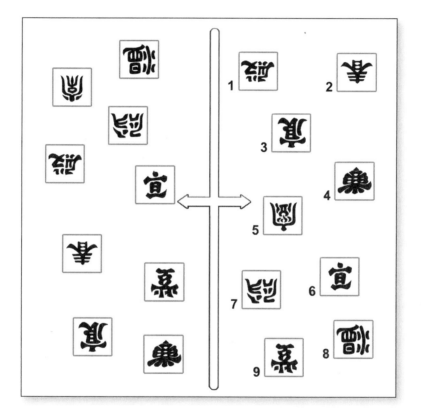

Working Both Sides

Take a careful look at these two sets of characters. Which characters appear in the series on the right but not in the series on the left?

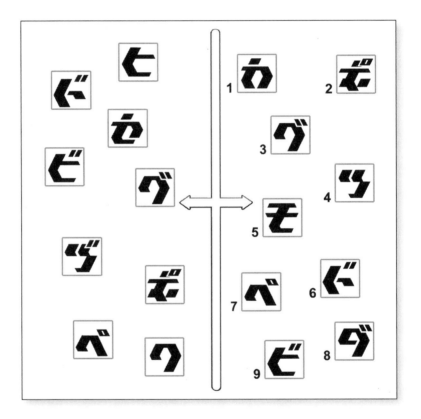

The Circuit Workout

Try to find the logical order of the pictures below.

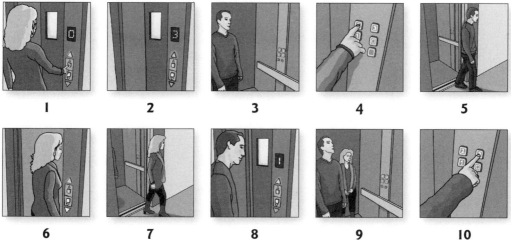

1 2 3 4 5

6 7 8 9 10

It Takes Two

Which two waiters are exactly alike?

It Takes Two

Which two rock stars are exactly alike?

Pencils Up

Link the eight black round figures without raising your pencil. You cannot touch the other figures, and you cannot go between two figures more than once.

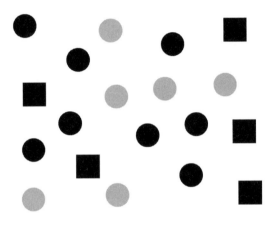

Pencils Up

Link the eight gray triangles without raising your pencil. You cannot touch the other figures, and you cannot go between two figures more than once.

Power Squats

Find a seven-letter word in the grid below. Letters must be adjacent to the next letter in the word.

G	M	U	E
P	R	A	F
E	G	H	Y
H	I	W	A

Power Squats

Find an eight-letter word in the grid below. Letters must be adjacent to the next letter in the word.

N	E	L	P
I	N	A	A
B	E	L	E
U	A	P	S

Power Squats

Find an eight-letter word in the grid below. Letters must be adjacent to the next letter in the word.

S	I	R	O
A	U	O	M
G	N	T	P
N	I	A	U

Power Squats

Find an eight-letter word in the grid below. Letters must be adjacent to the next letter in the word.

E	F	E	C
T	O	C	U
R	E	O	L
A	C	N	E

Power Squats

Find a nine-letter word in the grid below. Letters must be adjacent to the next letter in the word.

C	O	O	T
C	O	R	C
U	L	L	E
A	I	D	T

Resistance Training

Find the odd word in the following series, and justify your answer.

Houston	Miami	Montreal	Seattle	Chicago

The odd one is: _____

Celsius	Fahrenheit	Faraday	Kelvin	Reaumur

The odd one is: _____

Resistance Training

Find the odd word in the following series, and justify your answer.

Eurythmics	The Cranberries	Depeche Mode	The Police	Dire Straits

The odd one is: _____

Marco Polo	Jacques Cartier	Vasco de Gama	James Cook	Raffaello

The odd one is: _____

Resistance Training

Find the odd word in the following series, and justify your answer.

stetson	ballerina	high-heel	boot	moccasin

The odd one is: _____

bolete	eucalyptus	morel	chanterelle	truffle

The odd one is: _____

Resistance Training

Find the odd word in the following series, and justify your answer.

Everyone Says I Love You	Mighty Aphrodite	Annie Hall	The Godfather	Match Point

The odd one is: _____

Churchill	Franco	Thatcher	Blair	Wilson

The odd one is: _____

Resistance Training

Find the odd word in the following series, and justify your answer.

violin	tuba	horn	saxophone	trumpet

The odd one is: _____

trout	herring	shark	ray	tuna

The odd one is: _____

Muscle Groups

This list contains four adjectives and four nouns. Can you find them?

mad   clumsy   property   apple

big   helium   tired   loneliness

In this grid, classify words as adjectives or nouns and write them down in alphabetical order.

Adjectives	Nouns

Muscle Groups

This list contains four adjectives and four nouns. Can you find them?

man	honor	funny	weird
way	broken	old	furniture

In this grid, classify words as adjectives or nouns and write them down in alphabetical order.

Adjectives	Nouns

Conditioning

Classify the ten items in this list in two categories, and title each category.

Mediterranean	Caspian
Victoria	Bering
Ness	Baikal
Michigan	Red
China	Great Salt

Title: _____

Title: _____

Conditioning

Classify the ten items in this list in two categories, and title each category.

Southern		Mississippi
Atlantic		Amur
Arctic		Pacific
Amazon		Indian
Thames		Nile

Title: _____   **Title:** _____

Conditioning

Classify the ten items in this list in two categories, and title each category.

ton	mile
kilogram	stone
yard	feet
pound	inch
meter	ounce

Title: _____   **Title:** _____

Conditioning

Classify the ten items in this list in two categories, and title each category.

fluid ounce	liter
minute	quart
second	gallon
nanosecond	hour
pint	millisecond

Title: _____ **Title:** _____

Alignment

Find the word that corresponds to the definition.

1. mineralized or otherwise preserved remains or traces (such as footprints) of animals, plants, and other organisms

_____

2. ring with a flat bottom fixed on a leather strap, usually hung from each side of a saddle to create a footrest for the rider on a riding animal

_____

Alignment

Find the word that corresponds to the definition.

1. hard, rounded object produced by certain mollusks, primarily oysters

_____

2. digit of the foot of a human or animal

_____

Alignment

Find the word that corresponds to the definition.

1. shelter, consisting of sheets of fabric or other material draped over or attached to a frame of poles

_____

2. hair that grows on a man's chin, cheeks, and neck

_____

Alignment

Find the word that corresponds to the definition.

1. tracked armoured fighting vehicle, designed primarily to engage enemy forces by the use of direct fire

   _____

2. distinctive mark or impression made upon an object, most often paper, used to indicate the prepayment of a fee

   _____

Alignment

Find the word that corresponds to the definition.

1. religion and philosophy from ancient India based on the teachings of the Buddha

   _____

2. form of expression in which an implicit meaning is concealed or contradicted by the explicit meaning of the expression

   _____

Lateral Raises

The letters of the following words have been mixed up. They are all related to health. The first letter of each word is given as a clue.

ETBLAT: T _____

BESETAID: D _____

UEROIECSCENN: N _____

EAHTLHACRE: H _____

Lateral Raises

The letters of the following words have been mixed up. They are all related to health. The first letter of each word is given as a clue.

INATOIVCCAN: V_____

PTMOYSM: S_____

NEMIOTNT: O_____

RTORYABLAO: L_____

Lateral Raises

The letters of the following words have been mixed up. They are all related to health or architecture. The first letter of each word is given as a clue.

ENTSITRDY: D _____

IIEFWMD: M _____

GIINUBLD: B _____

IEOCRNC: C _____

Lateral Raises

The letters of the following words have been mixed up. They are all related to architecture. The first letter of each word is given as a clue.

MMDRISEON: M_____

LOCMNU: C_____

AABSIILC: B_____

OUVSSRIO: V_____

Lateral Raises

The letters of the following words have been mixed up. They are all related to architecture. The first letter of each word is given as a clue.

SKYTOENE: K_____

NNOOACDLE: C_____

YRPMIDA: P_____

SSCARPEYKR: S_____

Basketball in New York

Determine the minimum number of moves needed to move from the configuration in Figure A to the configuration in Figure B. Follow these rules:

- Balls may move out of baskets only upward.
- You may not place more than three balls in one basket.
- You may move only one ball at a time.

A

B

Basketball in New York

Determine the minimum number of moves needed to move from the configuration in Figure A to the configuration in Figure B. Follow these rules:

- Balls may move out of baskets only upward.
- You may not place more than three balls in one basket.
- You may move only one ball at a time.

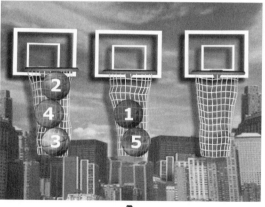

A

B

No Problem!

Solve this mathematical problem. If you need to, you can use a pencil and paper.

Every hour the kitchen clock gets five minutes faster. The living room clock gets five minutes slower every hour. They were both set at the same time. The kitchen clock displays 3:30 p.m., and the living room clock displays 12 p.m. What time is it?

No Problem!

Solve this mathematical problem. If you need to, you can use a pencil and paper.

Four friends have to go to the other side of the lake. They have only one boat, and this boat is big enough for only two rowers. Pete can cross one way in four minutes. It takes Mark twice as long. It takes Ivan twice as long as Mark. It takes Juliana twice as long as Ivan. Pete says they can do it in one hour.

When there are two rowers, the speed is that of the slowest. Is Pete correct? Explain your answer.

No Problem!

Solve this mathematical problem. If you need to, you can use a pencil and paper.

Eight bags are filled to 6/7 of their capacity with corn. Two-thirds are sold to a carrier. The carrier thinks he then needs six bags to put his corn in. Can the seller fill up the last two bags with the remaining corn?

No Problem!

Solve this mathematical problem. If you need to, you can use a pencil and paper.

At the dry cleaner, wire hangers are put at regular intervals on a round cable. Wire hangers are numbered, starting with 1. When wire hanger 8 is opposite wire hanger 15, then wire hanger 81 is opposite wire hanger 92. How many wire hangers are there on the cable?

No Mistakes Allowed

Find the correct spelling of each word among the three options.

hypoglicemia	hippoglycemia	hypoglycemia
circumstence	cyrcumstance	circumstance
enciclopedia	encyclopedia	encycloppedia
multilingual	multylingual	multilyngual

No Mistakes Allowed

Find the correct spelling of each word among the three options.

mathemmatics	mathematics	mathemattics
southestern	southeeastern	southeastern
asthma	athsma	athma
playwright	playright	pllaywright

No Mistakes Allowed

Find the correct spelling of each word among the three options.

psychotherapist	psichotherapist	psychotherrapist
ballistic	ballystic	balistic
conservattionist	conservationnist	conservationist
neuroscientist	neuroscyentist	neurroscientist

No Mistakes Allowed

Find the correct spelling of each word among the three options.

evollution	evvolution	evolution
conspirassy	conspiracy	connspiracy
session	sesson	sesion
breaststrok	brestroke	breaststroke

No Mistakes Allowed

Find the correct spelling of each word among each word among the three options.

searchablle	sercheable	searchable
geographiccally	geographically	geographicaly
domminance	dominnance	dominance
reluctanssy	relluctancy	reluctancy

No Mistakes Allowed

Find the correct spelling of each word among the three options.

amunition	amunnition	ammunition
contingent	continjent	continngent
invulnnerable	invulnerable	invulnerrable
sugestion	suggesstion	suggestion

No Mistakes Allowed

Find the correct spelling of each word among the three options.

incongruously	**incongrously**	**inkongruously**
government	**governement**	**goverment**
depyction	**deppiction**	**depiction**
aftermmath	**aftemath**	**aftermath**

Working Both Sides

Take a careful look at these two sets of characters. Which characters appear in the series on the right but not in the series on the left?

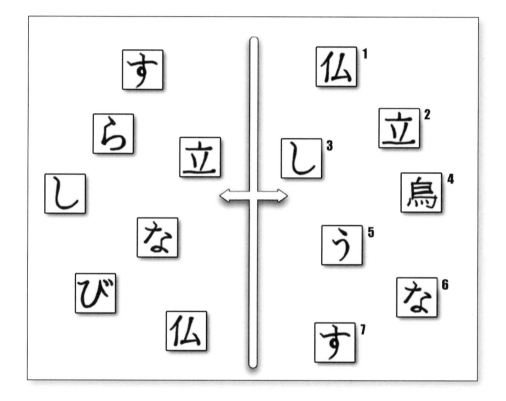

Working Both Sides

Take a careful look at these two sets of characters. Which characters appear in the series on the right but not in the series on the left?

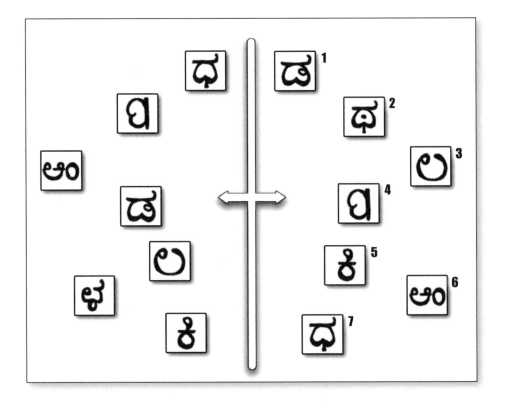

Interval Training

Can you put back together the ten three-part words that have been split and spread across the grid? Each part can be used only once, and the splits may not necessarily be the part splits you find in the dictionary.

HINT: *The theme is* **jobs and professions.**

tor	sear	fe	ger	cer
pro	ccount	cher	re	ter
pec	en	fi	ssist	di
pen	a	ins	gi	ant
neer	ssor	a	rec	ma
of	tor	na	ant	car

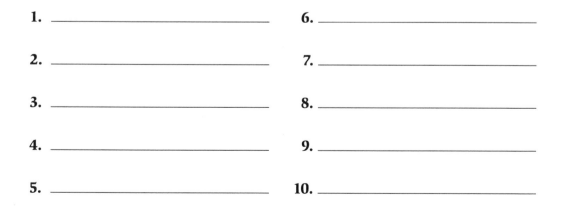

1. _____   6. _____

2. _____   7. _____

3. _____   8. _____

4. _____   9. _____

5. _____   10. _____

Interval Training

Can you put back together the ten three-part words that have been split and spread across the grid? Each part can be used only once, and the splits may not necessarily be the part splits you find in the dictionary.

HINT: *The theme is* **jobs and professions**

ar	cist	pist	bra	tect
na	gner	jour	per	de
phar	sult	ni	na	ant
a	tech	chi	con	lyst
li	bell	the	ra	cian
ma	si	list	rian	son

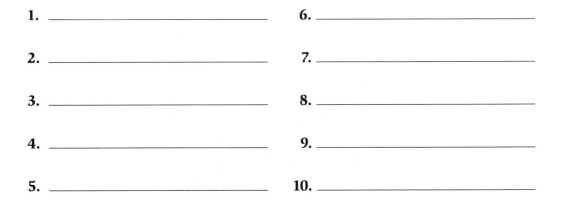

1. _____   6. _____

2. _____   7. _____

3. _____   8. _____

4. _____   9. _____

5. _____   10. _____

Combination Sets

Take a careful look at the nine elements below and try to determine which ones are not part of the larger figure. Beware, some elements may just have been turned around.

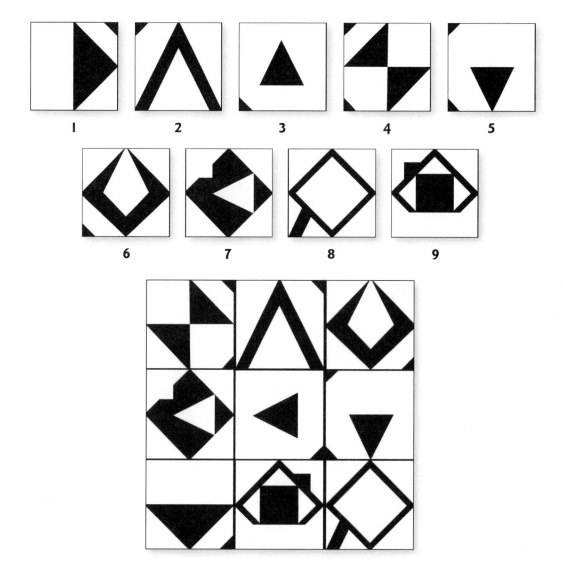

Combination Sets

Take a careful look at the nine elements below and try to determine which ones are not part of the larger figure. Beware, some elements may just have been turned around.

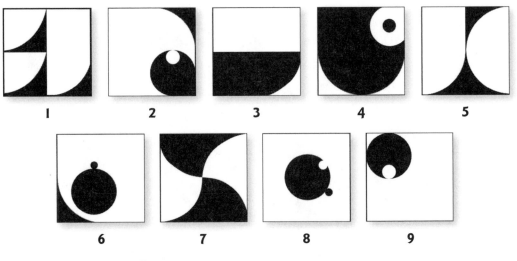

1 2 3 4 5

6 7 8 9

Distance Run

Take a careful look at the location of the nine objects in this landscape.

The image below shows the same landscape as seen from above. Determine where you would stand in the scenery to view the landscape as it appears in the image above.

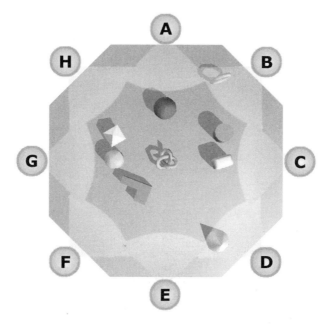

Distance Run

Take a careful look at the location of the nine objects in this landscape.

The image below shows the same landscape as seen from above. Determine where you would stand in the scenery to view the landscape as it appears in the image above.

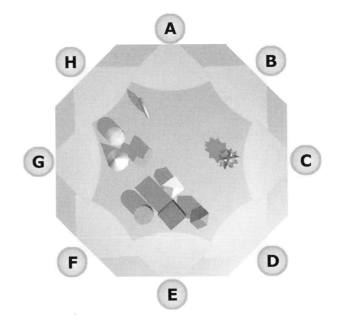

Cross Training

Decipher this quotation about life from Winston Churchill. Each symbol represents a letter, but it is always the same letter.

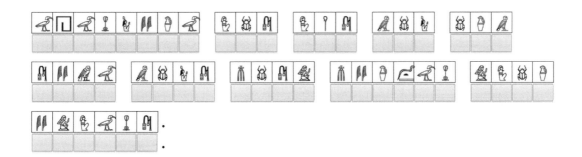

Cross Training

Decipher this quotation about life from John Ruskin. Each symbol represents a letter, but it is always the same letter.

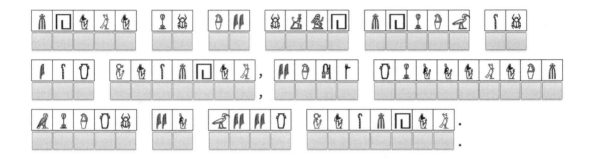

Cross Training

Decipher this quotation about life from Arthur Schopenhauer. Each symbol represents a letter, but it is always the same letter.

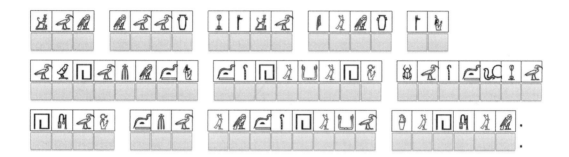

Cross Training

Decipher this quotation about life from Albert Einstein. Each symbol represents a letter, but it is always the same letter.

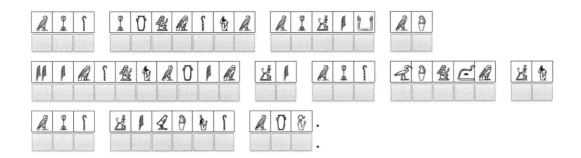

Reverse Crunches

Find the opposite of each of the words below. The first letter has been given as a clue.

affirmative: n_____

forward: b_____

below: a_____

Which word is not a synonym of the other four?

clueless   restless   fidgety   fretful   itchy

Reverse Crunches

Find the opposite of each of the words below. The first letter has been given as a clue.

1. night: d_____

2. pagan: r_____

3. shy: b_____

Which word is not a synonym of the other four?

highlight   sunlight   bring out   spotlight   play up

Reverse Crunches

Find the opposite of each of the words below. The first letter has been given as a clue.

1. face up: a_____

2. remember: f_____

3. tame: w_____

Which word is not a synonym of the other four?

godlike   divine   providential   elysian   divinity

Reverse Crunches

Find the opposite of each of the words below. The first letter has been given as a clue.

1. prevent: p_____

2. wise: f_____

3. handy: i_____

Which word is not a synonym of the other four?

    mobile   wondering   nomadic   peregrine   wandering

Reverse Crunches

Find the opposite of each of the words below. The first letter has been given as a clue.

1. homozygous: h_____

2. break: r_____

3. peace: w_____

Which word is not a synonym of the other four?

common   fabulous   terrific   extraordinary   amazing

Reverse Crunches

Find the opposite of each of the words below. The first letter has been given as a clue.

1. harmony: d_____

2. despair: h_____

3. smooth: r_____

Which word is not a synonym of the other four?

    dream   illusion   fantasy   fancy   truth

Maxing Out

Identify the nine differences between these two pictures.

Maxing Out

Identify the nine differences between these two pictures.

Working the Memory Muscle

Take a minute to memorize the 10 words below without looking at the bottom half of the page.

nullification   chacha   sure-fire   dockage   publicity

tutu   gardening   hoover   step   bathroom

Now cover up the list of words and answer the following questions:

1. Which of the words are related to the theme "Dance"?

_____

2. Which, if any, words on the list are compound words?

_____

3. Which of the words comes first alphabetically?

_____

4. Which word has the most letters?

_____

5. Which, if any, of the words are related to the theme "Home"?

_____

Working the Memory Muscle

Take a minute to memorize the 10 words below without looking at the bottom half of the page.

negligee   tutelary   babysitter   aficionado   dolce vita

turtleneck   baccarat   wit   poaching   liaison

Now cover up the list of words and answer the following questions:

1. How many foreign words are there on the list? Which are they?

_____

2. What are the two shortest words?

_____

3. Are there any names of games? If so, which ones?

_____

4. Which words have in some way to do with animals?

_____

5. Do you remember any abstract words? Which?

_____

Can You Spot Me?

Find the odd one in this series.

HINT: *The odd one is* ▶◀.

Can You Spot Me?

Find the odd one in this series.

HINT: *The odd one is* 🏔.

Can You Spot Me?

Find the odd one in this series.

PLTFIONGUCREFUQYWBFYZFEUYXZOUIAIOZWODZWEDIZCNTREYUSN8B
UEUORFORZUXUIUOEZQXPPQUZENCAMZ9RUCNANUC8EUR4NURZQ7ER
YCBZ7YQ32Q87P94VP32A45Q409VH6V09Z65C94Z9EZICQZIOR39CQ23N85
X7Q465BQ5X367B235V7N374NNVZ098BJTD09CZ34980Q9N78B2NB87BQVB
37518N54V6VQ540484V6B7VQ4MYBTFBLNWE4BYUVXQBTAEQTYVZW9EZR
YCNS9TUVTYNREXWURIROXQVITPEPSIRTCYEUBHUYNUUTFTCC65REZW

HINT: *The odd one is* 1.

Can You Spot Me?

Find the odd one in this series.

71625341693049507643716145039695594031374652623541254965674596572
31569754265963545669745654723515236005520145902570364501230095674
56032590210805463059657420321025630025696523014752012302502365965
47203021475021563096523014575421201236957659541230001235566965745
15263292125457102563402512043205696523054127059635062145709502630
05147754236950069563254175263956265412100745996536921123564700525

HINT: *The odd one is* 8.

Can You Spot Me?

Find the odd one in this series.

HINT: *The odd one is* .

Cooling Down

Are the following statements right or wrong?

1. The true name of James Dean is James Francis Dean.

2. The patella is a bone in the knee.

3. A wishbone boom is an accessory used in windsurfing.

4. The Yalta Conference was held in 1944.

5. There were four Brontë sisters.

Cooling Down

Are the following statements right or wrong?

1. Amethyst is a purple variety of quartz.

2. The flag of Norway is yellow and blue.

3. *Moby-Dick* is the story of a nice whale.

4. The square root of 144 is 12.

5. The National Geographic Society was founded in 1888.

Cooling Down

Are the following statements right or wrong?

1. Black tea contains caffeine.

2. *Wuthering Heights* was written by Emily Brontë.

3. The twist is a dance from the 1980s.

4. Brass is a copper-zinc alloy.

5. The word *totem* is of Native American origin.

Cooling Down

Are the following statements right or wrong?

1. Harrison Ford starred in *Hook*.

2. *Trapezium* is a word used for both a bone and a muscle.

3. The painter Jean-Michel Basquiat died in a car accident.

4. Dolphins are fish.

5. Verse writing uses meter.

No Pain, No _____

Can you supply the beginning words of each of the following proverbs?

1. _____ that feeds you.

2. _____ in the mouth.

3. _____ twice shy.

No Pain, No _____

Can you supply the beginning words of each of the following proverbs?

1. _____ will be boys.

2. _____ travels fast.

3. _____ rules the world.

No Pain, No _____

Can you supply the beginning words of each of the following proverbs?

1. _____ by its cover.

2. _____ like an old fool.

3. _____ doesn't buy happiness.

Easy Puzzles

No Pain, No _____
1. **One man's loss** is another man's gain.
2. **Actions speak** louder than words.
3. **Finders keepers,** losers weepers.

No Pain, No _____
1. **Silence** is golden.
2. **To err** is human.
3. **God helps** those who help themselves.

No Pain, No _____
1. **A stitch in time** saves nine.
2. **Seeing** is believing.
3. **Experience is** the mother of all wisdom.

No Pain, No _____
1. **Like father,** like son.
2. **Cleanliness is next** to godliness.
3. **Home is where** the heart is.

Entangled Figures
Figures 2, 6, and 9 are part of the image.

Entangled Figures
Figures 1, 3, and 5 are part of the image.

Entangled Figures
Figures 3, 5, and 8 are part of the image.

All-Star Game
1. SPATULA
2. COTTAGE
3. CONTACT
4. TRACHEA
5. TETANUS
6. EXHAUST

All-Star Game
1. ALEWIFE
2. MINIBUS
3. MYSTERY
4. CABBAGE
5. CANASTA
6. SUAVITY

All-Star Game
1. WHISPER
2. HEATHER
3. HEROINE
4. SCHOLAR
5. SPARROW
6. RELAPSE

All-Star Game
1. SOILAGE
2. AERIALS
3. ALEWIFE
4. PRAIRIE
5. PARSECS
6. SURFACE

Towers of Hanoi
At least four moves are needed to move from A to B.

Towers of Hanoi
At least six moves are needed to move from A to B.

Towers of Hanoi
At least five moves are needed to move from A to B.

Easy as One-Two-Three
There are twenty squares in this figure (eleven small ones, seven medium ones, one big one, one overarching one).

Easy as One-Two-Three
There are nine squares in this figure (five small ones, three medium ones, one overarching one).

Easy as One-Two-Three
There are nineteen squares in this figure (two extra-small ones, eleven small ones, three medium ones, two big ones, one overarching one).

Can You Spot Me?
Line 3, fifth from the left

Can You Spot Me?
Line 1, second from the left

Can You Spot Me?
Line 4, second from right

Warming Up
She was so deceptive that no one could guess **sh**e was actually cheating all the time, and that her prudi**sh** looks hid **sh**ameful behaviors that only **sh**e knew. **Sh**e was capable of going to church and confessing the most hideous sins to the priest without feeling a**sh**amed. Her friends were quite **s**ure **sh**e was of an honest nature, and that **sh**e was a perfect match with Andy, the charming boy whom all the young ladies fell for.

Warming Up
Bob drank his co**ff**ee then silently prayed **f**or things to go smoothly. He **f**elt the easy **ph**ase of bringing the girl back home was just the **f**irst step o**f** many harder ones, and that i**f** she did not **f**eel sa**f**e here, she would **f**lee once again, with only a **f**ew chances to **f**ind her quickly. This was a rou**gh** world, and the pictures o**f** the happy days that should have brought joy to his **f**ear-stricken heart could not help much.

Incomplete Workout
The missing tile is 1.

Incomplete Workout
The missing tile is 3.

Hidden Strength

Hidden Strength

Working Both Sides
The characters that can be found only on the right are 2, 3, and 7.

Working Both Sides
The characters that can be found only on the right are 4 and 6.

The Circuit Workout
3, 6, 1, 2, 4, 5

It Takes Two
The two perfectly identical characters are 3 and 7. The details that could enable you to delete the other pictures are:
#1: The end of the umbrella is not visible.
#2: The umbrella does not have any stripes.
#4: The foot of the character is missing.
#5: The stem of the umbrella is more visible in the hand of the geisha.
#6: There is no ribbon in the geisha's hair.
#8: A part of the geisha's belt is missing.
#9: Floral patterns are missing on the kimono.

It Takes Two
The two perfectly identical characters are 2 and 9. The details that could enable you to delete the other pictures are:
#1: There is less black on the stork's feathers.
#3: The inferior part of the beak is missing.
#4: The joint is missing on the stork's right foot.
#5: The gray part is black.
#6: The straw strands are missing from the nest.
#7: An egg is missing.
#8: The black end of the stork's wing is missing.

Pencils Up
There are several solutions.

Spinning Class
The two figures are mirror images.

Spinning Class
The two figures are identical.

Resistance Training
The odd one is the Rockefeller Center. It is the only American monument among four British ones.

The odd one is the scalpel. It is the only surgeon's tool among four gardener's tools.

Resistance Training
The odd one is Michael Shumacher. He is the only F1 pilot among four basketball players.

The odd one is the Sun. It is the only star among four planets.

Resistance Training
The odd one is the snail. It is the only mollusk among four crustaceans.

The odd one is *The Wall*. It is the only Pink Floyd song among four movies by Marilyn Monroe.

Resistance Training
The odd one is cod. It is the only fish among four meats.

The odd one is fir. It is the only softwood tree among four hardwood ones.

Resistance Training
The odd one is Tom Cruise. He is the only actor among four writers.

The odd one is Morocco. It is the only African country among four European countries.

Power Squats
FURRIER

Power Squats
TOURISM

Power Squats
PROPERTY

Power Squats
MOISTURE

Power Squats
PRINCESS

Power Squats
ARCHIVE

Power Squats
REPTILE

Power Squats
COMPANY

The Proper Form
1. right   2. right   3. right

The Proper Form
1. left   2. left   3. right

The Proper Form
1. left   2. right   3. right

The Proper Form
1. right   2. left   3. right

The Proper Form
1. left   2. right   3. left

The Proper Form
1. right   2. left   3. right

The Proper Form
1. right   2. left   3. left

The Proper Form
1. right   2. left   3. right

Muscle Memory
1. C   4. B
2. A   5. D
3. E

Muscle Memory
1. D   4. E
2. C   5. B
3. A

Muscle Memory
1. D   4. A
2. E   5. C
3. B

Muscle Memory
1. B   4. A
2. E   5. C
3. D

Working Both Sides
The image that can be found only on the right is 5.

Working Both Sides
The images that can be found only on the right are 3 and 7.

Interval Training
tunic, sandal, sweatpants, bowtie, robe, trousers, sweater, jumper, blouse, denim

Interval Training
stocking, poncho, mitten, glove, jacket, garment, swimsuit, raincoat, collar, knickers

Interval Training
rhythm, tango, salsa, ballet, tutu, rumba, solo, polka, fox-trot, mambo

Interval Training
chacha, go-go, ballroom, tempo, hip-hop, slipper, footwork, pointe, stage, scene

Combination Sets
Square 3 is not used in the combined image.

Combination Sets
All squares are used in the combined image.

Distance Run
The landscape is seen from point D.

Distance Run
The landscape is seen from point D.

Cross Training
Popularity is the crown of laurel that the world puts on bad art.

Cross Training
I must place on record my regret that the human race ever learned to fly.

Cross Training
All my life I wanted to be someone; I guess I should have been more specific.

Cross Training
The natural role of twentieth century man is anxiety.

Reverse Crunches
beautiful - ugly
rich - poor
close - open

Problematic is not a synonym of the four other words.

Reverse Crunches
long - short
discreet - indiscreet
forbidden - allowed

Tell is not a synonym of the four other words.

Reverse Crunches
true - false
accept - reject
admirable - despicable

Meditate is not a synonym of the four other words.

Reverse Crunches
small - big
raw - cooked
complicate - simplify

Tranquil is not a synonym of the four other words.

Reverse Crunches
busy - idle
easy - hard
careful - careless

Rigid is not a synonym of the four other words.

Reverse Crunches
increasing - decreasing
empty - full
less - more

Pride is not a synonym of the four other words.

Maxing Out

Maxing Out

Working the Memory Muscle

1. The animals on the list are **elephant**, **cow**, and **shrimp**.

2. The abstract words are **design** and **part**.

3. **Cow** is the shortest word on the list.

Working the Memory Muscle

1. **Tea** is the drink on the list.

2. The profession named on the list is **chef**.

3. A **feather** can be found on a bird.

Can You Spot Me?
Line 3, ninth from the left

Can You Spot Me?
Line 3, twenty-first from the left

Can You Spot Me?
Line 6, fourth from the left

Can You Spot Me?
Line 4, third from the left

Can You Spot Me?
Line 5, second from the left

Can You Spot Me?
Line 3, third from the left

Can You Spot Me?
Line 2, second from the right

Cooling Down
1. Wrong   4. Right
2. Right   5. Right
3. Wrong

Cooling Down
1. Right   4. Right
2. Wrong   5. Wrong
3. Wrong

Cooling Down
1. Right   4. Wrong
2. Right   5. Right
3. Right

Cooling Down
1. Wrong   4. Right
2. Wrong   5. Right
3. Wrong

Cooling Down
1. Right   4. Wrong
2. Right   5. Right
3. Wrong

Cooling Down
1. Wrong   4. Wrong
2. Wrong   5. Wrong
3. Right

Cooling Down
1. Right   4. Right
2. Wrong   5. Wrong
3. Right

No Pain, No _____
1. **Curiosity** killed the cat.
2. **An apple a day keeps** the doctor away.
3. **Play it** by ear.

No Pain, No _____
1. **A chain is no stronger than** its weakest link.
2. **A fool and his money** are soon parted.
3. **Ask me no questions** and hear no lies.

No Pain, No _____
1. **Beauty is** only skin deep.
2. **Beggars** can't be choosers.
3. **It's raining** cats and dogs.

No Pain, No _____
1. **Don't count your chickens** before they are hatched.
2. **You reap** what you sow.
3. **Fight fire** with fire.

Medium Puzzles

No Pain, No _____
1. **The early bird** catches the worm.
2. **Watch out for** number one.
3. **Life is just** a bowl of cherries.

No Pain, No _____
1. **United we stand,** divided we fall.
2. **Too many cooks** spoil the broth.
3. **The end** justifies the means.

Entangled Figures
Figures 3, 6, and 8 are part of the image.

Entangled Figures
Figures 1, 2, and 9 are part of the image.

Entangled Figures
Figures 4, 5, and 9 are part of the image.

Entangled Figures
Figures 5, 7, and 9 are part of the image.

Towers of Hanoi
At least nine moves are needed move from A to B.

Towers of Hanoi
At least eleven moves are needed to move from A to B.

Easy as One-Two-Three
There are twenty triangles in this figure.

Easy as One-Two-Three
There are eighteen triangles in this figure.

Easy as One-Two-Three
There are eighteen triangles in this figure.

Throwing a Curve

The three strange elements are:

- Ms. Cole couldn't have driven her son to school if her car was packed from the passengers's seat to the trunk.
- She couldn't have looked in her rearview mirror for the same reason.
- Her son wouldn't be going to school on Christmas day.

Throwing a Curve

The three strange elements are:

- Caroline was hired in August, so there wouldn't be snow outside.
- The building has five floors, so the fourth cannot be the top.
- No book can be more than seven centuries old, because printing had not been invented at that point.

Can You Spot Me?

Line 2, third from the left

Can You Spot Me?

Line 3, fifth from the left

Warming Up

She d*i*d not really have the choice anyway. The tw*o* of them had decided the boy would fin*i*sh sch*oo*l s*oo*n. The fr*ui*t of all her efforts could be r*u*ined *if* the r*u*les were not respected, she thought. What g*oo*d was there *i*n trying to find h*i*m a job *if* he was going t*o* have h*i*s f*oo*l*i*sh behavior again, as s*oo*n as he was out of h*i*s r*oo*m? Th*i*s sol*u*tion was as s*ui*table as going out w*i*th a fl*u* under pouring rain. She t*oo* had her opinion about th*i*s, and one that d*i*d not need pr*oo*fing: *i*t came straight from experience. When he gr*e*w older, he would understand.

Warming Up

The dentist's f*a*ce looked tense. The man had tr*ie*d to m*a*ke his best, but he clearly needed a br*ea*k. The heat was gr*ea*t too, and many fl*ie*s also took a close look at the oper*a*tion. The pr*i*ce to p*ay* was h*i*gh, as the horse could d*ie* from the surgery, and it was not the k*i*nd of horse that one could f*i*nd every d*ay*. This one had won many r*a*ces, and the d*ay* of the Grand National, you could hear people pr*ay*, so s*i*lent was the audience. The owner, a br*a*ve man from Colorado, had ch*a*sed for years before finding the horse of his l*i*fe. His w*i*fe had left long ago, and all that rem*ai*ned from her now was memories.

Incomplete Workout

The missing tile is 4.

Incomplete Workout

The missing tile is 3.

Hidden Strength

Hidden Strength

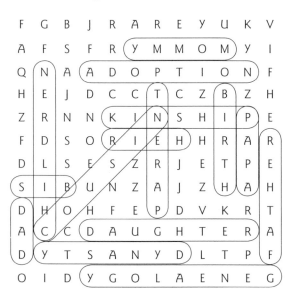

Working Both Sides
The characters that can be found only on the right are 1, 4, and 6.

Working Both Sides
The characters that can be found only on the right are 5 and 8.

The Circuit Workout
6, 3, 8, 2, 5, 1, 4, 7

It Takes Two
The two perfectly identical characters are 4 and 7. The details that could enable you to delete the other pictures are:
#1: A tuft of hair is missing on the dragon's head.
#2: The tip of the dragon's tail is missing.
#3: A claw is missing.
#5: The eyes are black.
#6: Part of the spine crest is missing on the back.
#8: Teeth are missing.
#9: Black lines are missing on the wings.

It Takes Two
The two perfectly identical characters are 6 and 9. The details that could enable you to delete the other pictures are:
#1: Buttons are missing on his jacket.
#2: Stripes are missing.
#3: The badge is missing on his jacket.
#4: The whistle is missing.
#5: The badge is missing on his cap.
#7: The belt buckle is missing.
#8: The gun's case is missing.

Pencil's Up Solution
There are several solutions.

Power Squats
EYELASH

Power Squats
SECURITY

Power Squats
PRINTERS

Power Squats
ARRIVAL

Solo or Group Exercise?

Singular	Plural
box	children
criterion	foxes
nail	glasses
sock	stairs

Solo or Group Exercise?

Singular	Plural
cheese	feet
hemisphere	geese
shoe	sketches
tribe	women

Solo or Group Exercise?

Singular	Plural
bear	halves
crane	people
eyelash	sins
silver	teeth

Solo or Group Exercise?

Singular	Plural
city	mice
excess	prices
mouse	supplies
speed	thieves

Conditioning

Martial arts	Team sports
aïkido	basketball
judo	soccer
karate	handball
Thai-boxing	rugby
tae kwon do	volleyball

Conditioning

Winter sports	Water sports
bobsledding	water-skiing
ice hockey	surfing
mountaineering	sailing
skiing	windsurfing
snowboarding	wakeboarding

Conditioning

Literary authors	Modern bands
Henry James	The Rolling Stones
Nathaniel Hawthorne	Pink Floyd
Francis Scott Fitzgerald	Texas
John Irving	Black Eyed Peas
James Joyce	The Doors

Conditioning

Classical composers	Painters
Mozart	Leonardo Da Vinci
Debussy	Salvador Dali
Berlioz	J. M. Basquiat
Schubert	Andy Warhol
Chopin	Lucian Freud

Alignment
1. diameter 2. pasta

Alignment
1. dynasty 2. pen

Alignment
1. silhouette 2. manga

Alignment
1. dam 2. chess

Alignment
1. diabetes 2. rabbits

Lateral Raises
SHOOTING; CAMERA; ACTRESS; CASTING

Lateral Raises
ANIMATION; SUBTITLES; DIALOGUE; SCENARIO

Lateral Raises
DIRECTOR; SOUNDTRACK; FORECAST; TEMPERATURE

Lateral Raises
FAHRENHEIT; ATMOSPHERE; CLIMATE; SUNLIGHT

Lateral Raises
TORNADO; HURRICANE; SATELLITE; BAROMETER

Basketball in New York

You need at least four moves to go from A to B:

- ball 1 in basket 1
- ball 2 in basket 2
- ball 1 in basket 3
- ball 5 in basket 3

Basketball in New York

You need at least five moves to go from A to B:

- ball 1 in basket 3
- ball 3 in basket 3
- ball 4 in basket 3
- ball 2 in basket 2
- ball 4 in basket 1

No Problem!

Convert all the measures in feet, and then do the following calculations:

$25 \times 10 = 250$
$30 \times 8.33 = 249.9$
$7 \times 7 = 49$

The total length is 548.9 feet.

No Problem!

On day thirty-nine, the algae covers half the pool.

On day thirty-eight, the algae covers half this surface, which is one-quarter.

Therefore, the algae needs thirty-eight days to cover a quarter of the surface of the pool.

No Problem!

$5 \div 100 \times 25,000 = \$1,250$

The first car seller offers a discount of $1,250.

$4 \div 100 \times 22,000 = \$880$

The second car seller offers a discount of $880.

The biggest discount is the one offered by the first car seller.

$25,000 - 1,250 = \$23,750$

With the discount, the first model costs $23,750.

$22,000 - 880 = \$21,120$

With the discount, the second model costs $21,120.

The cheapest vehicle, with or without a discount, remains the second one.

No Problem!

Mister Martin has only four jam jars—one of each flavor!

No Mistakes Allowed

constitutional; harmony; comedy; millionaire

No Mistakes Allowed

obsolete; armament; literally; multiplicity

No Mistakes Allowed

currently; elephant; sustainability; cowardice

No Mistakes Allowed

atmosphere; furniture; strawberry; impressive

No Mistakes Allowed

loyalty; expression; parallel; medicine

No Mistakes Allowed

disagreement; humiliation; powerfully; orchestra

Spinning Class

Figures 1 and 2 are identical, and figure 3 is a mirror image.

Spinning Class
Figures 1 and 2 are identical, and figure 3 is a mirror image.

Muscle Memory
1. D
2. B
3. E
4. A
5. C

Muscle Memory
1. B
2. C
3. D
4. E
5. A

Muscle Memory
1. C
2. D
3. B
4. E
5. A

Muscle Memory
1. D
2. A
3. E
4. B
5. C

Muscle Memory
1. A
2. C
3. E
4. B
5. D
v

Muscle Memory
1. A
2. C
3. E
4. B
5. D

Muscle Memory
1. B
2. D
3. E
4. A
5. C

Muscle Memory
1. B
2. A
3. D
4. E
5. C

Working Both Sides
The image that can be found only on the right is 4.

Working Both Sides
The image that can be found only on the right is 3.

Interval Training
euphoria, jealousy, modesty, bravery, courage, affection, pleasure, desire, seduction, patience

Interval Training
happiness, outrage, misery, surprise, affliction, distaste, dreadfulness, tenderness, sentiment, sensation

Interval Training
elephant, giraffe, vulture, caribou, gorilla, kangaroo, canary, pelican, cockatoo, mosquito

Interval Training
hyena, buffalo, koala, chimpanzee, octopus, crocodile, flamingo, anteater, leopard, lovebird

Combination Sets
All squares are used in the combined image.

Combination Sets
Squares 1 and 2 are not used in the combined image.

Distance Run
The landscape is seen from point E.

Distance Run
The landscape is seen from point H.

Cross Training
Give me the luxuries of life, and I will willingly do without the necessities.

Cross Training
When love turns into dust, money becomes the substitution.

Cross Training
Moderation is a fatal thing. Nothing succeeds like excess.

Cross Training
You can't be truly rude until you understand good manners.

Working the Memory Muscle
1. **Information** is the word that cannot be used in the plural.
2. There are two abstract words: **marriage** and **information**.
3. **Bear**, **boat**, and **jam** can be both a noun and a verb.
4. **Jam** and **cocoa** are edible.

Working the Memory Muscle
1. The colors **purple** and **brown** are one the list.
2. There are **no fruits** on the list.
3. The abstract words are **brown**, **particularity**, **vanity**, **purple**, and **hurry**.
4. **Jersey** is the name of a state.

Can You Spot Me?
Line 4, fifth from the left

Can You Spot Me?
Line 4, first from the right

Can You Spot Me?
Line 4, fourth from the left

Can You Spot Me?
Line 4, third from the right

Can You Spot Me?
Line 3, second from the left

Can You Spot Me?
Line 4, second from the right

Can You Spot Me?
Line 2, third from the right

Can You Spot Me?
Line 4, fifteenth from the left

No Pain, No _____
1. **Better late** than never.
2. **Ignorance** is bliss.
3. **A force to be** reckoned with.

No Pain, No _____
1. **Absence makes the heart** grow fonder.
2. **Don't mix business** with pleasure.
3. **Get up** and go.

No Pain, No _____
1. **Laughter is** the best medicine.
2. **Robbing Peter** to pay Paul.
3. **No good deed** goes unpunished.

No Pain, No _____
1. **You can't have your cake** and eat it too.
2. **Never** say never.
3. **One good turn** deserves another.

Hard Puzzles

No Pain, No _____

1. **Easy come,** easy go.
2. **The enemy** of my enemy is my friend.
3. **Good fences** make good neighbors.

No Pain, No _____

1. **Don't put all your eggs** in one basket.
2. **You can't see the forest** for the trees.
3. **Don't cut off your nose** to spite your face.

Entangled Figures

Figures 2, 4, and 6 are part of the image.

All-Star Game

1. TYPHOON
2. SULFATE
3. STEEPLE
4. STATION
5. SOLVENT
6. EPISODE

All-Star Game

1. GRAVITY
2. BREADTH
3. BRIGADE
4. MODESTY
5. MEETING
6. HOSPICE

All-Star Game

1. EDITION
2. ARSENIC
3. AVARICE
4. DENDRON
5. DISEASE
6. CARBINE

All-Star Game

1. SUICIDE
2. SURFING
3. SALSIFY
4. SOILAGE
5. SURPLUS
6. GRAVITY

Towers of Hanoi

At least nine moves are needed to move from A to B.

Towers of Hanoi

At least seven moves are needed to move from A to B.

Towers of Hanoi

At least fourteen moves are needed to move from A to B.

Easy as One-Two-Three

There are ten squares and twenty-four triangles in this figure.

Easy as One-Two-Three

There are fifteen squares and thirty-seven triangles in this figure.

Throwing a Curve

The four strange elements are:

- A Friesian is not a race horse; it's a show horse.
- If the horse is young, there is no reason for him to retire from competition.
- There are only thirty days in April.
- There are no dead leaves in April.

Throwing a Curve

The four strange elements are:

- Flights from Dallas to Sydney take more than six hours.
- The couple is on a honeymoon, so Mary is Dave's wife, not his fiancée.

- Pandas are not native to Australia.
- The honeymoon is said to last three weeks, but they are showing photographs to their friends a week later.

Can You Spot Me?
Line 5, thirteenth from the left

Can You Spot Me?
Line 3, sixteenth from the left

Can You Spot Me?
Line 5, second from the right

Incomplete Workout
The missing tiles are 3 and 4.

Incomplete Workout
The missing tiles are 1 and 2.

Hidden Strength

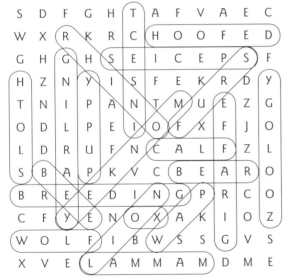

Hidden Strength

Working Both Sides
The character that can be found only on the right is 5.

Working Both Sides
The characters that can be found only on the right are 1, 4, 5, and 8.

The Circuit Workout
1, 6, 4, 8, 10, 9, 7, 3, 5, 2

It Takes Two
The two perfectly identical characters are 1 and 8. The details that could enable you to delete the other pictures are:

#2: The badge is missing from the vest.
#3: The hat has no stripe.
#4: Buttons are missing on the waiter's shirt.
#5: The napkin is longer.
#6: A glass is missing.
#7: The bow tie is missing.
#9: The right hand is missing.

It Takes Two
The two perfectly identical characters are 4 and 5. The details that could enable you to delete the other pictures are:
#1: The pegs are missing on the guitar's neck.
#2: The tattoo is missing on his right arm.
#3: The hand is missing on the guitar.
#6: The man's neck chain is missing.
#7: The tuft of hair on the top of his head is shorter.
#8: A tuft of hair is missing on the front of his head.
#9: The black part of the guitar is white.

Pencil's Up
There are several solutions.

Power Squats
HIGHWAY

Power Squats
SEAPLANE

Power Squats
MOUNTAIN

Power Squats
CONCERTO

Power Squats
COLLECTOR

Resistance Training
The odd one is Montreal—the only Canadian city among four American ones.

The odd one is Faraday, which is not a temperature measure.

Resistance Training
The odd one is The Cranberries—the only Irish band among four British bands.

The odd one is Raffaello—the only painter among four explorers.

Resistance Training
The odd one is stetson—the only hat among four types of shoes.

The odd one is eucalyptus—the only tree among four mushrooms.

Resistance Training
The odd one is *The Godfather*—the only film not directed by Woody Allen.

The odd one is Franco—the only Spanish leader among four British prime ministers.

Resistance Training
The odd one is violin. It is the only string instrument among four wind instruments.

The odd one is trout. It is the only freshwater fish among four saltwater fish.

Muscle Groups

Adjectives	Nouns
big	apple
clumsy	helium
mad	loneliness
tired	property

Muscle Groups

Adjectives	Nouns
broken	furniture
funny	honor
old	man
weird	way

Conditioning

Seas	Lakes
Caspian	Victoria
Red	Ness
Mediterranean	Baikal
Bering	Michigan
China	Great Salt

Conditioning

Oceans	Rivers
Southern	Amazon
Atlantic	Thames
Arctic	Mississippi
Pacific	Amur
Indian	Nile

Conditioning

Weight	Length
ton	mile
stone	yard
ounce	feet
pound	inch
kilogram	meter

Conditioning

Duration	Liquid measure
minute	quart
second	gallon
hour	pint
millisecond	liter
nanosecond	fluid ounce

Alignment
1. fossil   2. stirrup

Alignment
1. pearl   2. toe

Alignment
1. tent   2. beard

Alignment
1. tank   2. stamp

Alignment
1. Buddhism   2. irony

Lateral Raises
TABLET; DIABETES; NEUROSCIENCE; HEALTHCARE

Lateral Raises
VACCINATION; SYMPTOM; OINTMENT; LABORATORY

Lateral Raises
DENTISTRY; MIDWIFE; BUILDING; CORNICE

Lateral Raises
MODERNISM; COLUMN; BASILICA; VOUSSOIR

Lateral Raises
KEYSTONE; COLONNADE; PYRAMID; SKYSCRAPER

Basketball in New York
You need at least seven moves to go from A to B:
- ball 2 in basket 3
- ball 4 in basket 3
- ball 1 in basket 3
- ball 5 in basket 2
- ball 3 in basket 2
- ball 1 in basket 1
- ball 3 in basket 1

Basketball in New York
You need at least eight moves to go from A to B:
- ball 1 in basket 3
- ball 2 in basket 3
- ball 4 in basket 3
- ball 3 in basket 2
- ball 4 in basket 1
- ball 3 in basket 1
- ball 5 in basket 3
- ball 3 in basket 2

No Problem!

5 + 5 = 10

After each hour, the discrepancy grows 10 additional minutes. 3:30 p.m. – 12 p.m. = 3 hours and 30 minutes

Now the discrepancy is 3 hours and 30 minutes—i.e., 210 minutes.
210 ÷ 10 = 21

It has been 21 hours since the clocks were set.

21 × 5 = 105

Therefore, the clock in the kitchen is 105 minutes early; that in the living room is 105 minutes late—i.e., 1 hour and 45 minutes.

12 p.m. + 1 hour and 45 minutes = 1:45 p.m.

3:30 p.m. – 1 hour and 45 minutes = 1:45 p.m.

It is therefore 1:45 p.m.

No Problem!

Here is the fastest solution:

Pete and Mark must leave first.

2 × 4 = 8

It will take them 8 minutes.

Then Peter, the faster of the two, brings the boat back in 4 minutes.

Then Ivan and Juliana go.

8 × 2 × 2 = 32

It takes them 32 minutes.

The fastest of the three, Mark, brings the boat back in 8 minutes.

Then Pete and Mark cross again in 8 minutes.

8 + 4 + 32 + 8 + 8 = 60

So it takes the four friends 60 minutes to cross the river, which is indeed one hour. Therefore, Pete was right!

No Problem!

If y is the volume of corn that can be put in a bag, the initial volume of corn is:

6 ÷ 7 × y × 8

After the sale, one-third of the corn remains:

1/3 × 6/7 × y × 8 = 16/7 × y corn

and 16/7 = 2.3

2.3 > 2

So two bags are not enough to store the remaining corn.

No Problem!

If wire hangers 8 and 15 cross each other that means that the wire hanger that is half their way on the cable is at one end of the cable. It is wire hanger 12.

Also, if wire hangers 81 and 92 cross each other that means that the wire hanger that is half their way on the cable is at the other end of the cable. It is wire hanger 87.

87 – 12 = 75

The two wire hangers, each at one end of the cable, are 75 wire hangers apart.

75 × 2 = 150

Therefore, there are 150 wire hangers on the cable.

No Mistakes Allowed

hypoglycemia; circumstance; encyclopedia; multilingual

No Mistakes Allowed

mathematics; southeastern; asthma; playwright

No Mistakes Allowed

psychotherapist; ballistic; conservationist; neuroscientist

No Mistakes Allowed

evolution; conspiracy; session; breaststroke

No Mistakes Allowed

searchable; geographically; dominance; reluctancy

No Mistakes Allowed

ammunition; contingent; invulnerable; suggestion

No Mistakes Allowed

incongruously; government; depiction; aftermath

Working Both Sides

The images that can be found only on the right are 4 and 5.

Working Both Sides

The image that can be found only on the right is 2.

Interval Training

officer, professor, carpenter, director, inspector, engineer, researcher, manager, accountant, assistant

Interval Training

bellperson, architect, pharmacist, journalist, consultant, librarian, technician, therapist, analyst, designer

Combination Sets

Squares 4, 6, and 9 are not used in the combined image.

Combination Sets

Squares 3, 4, and 6 are not used in the combined image.

Distance Run

The landscape is seen from point G.

Distance Run

The landscape is seen from point H.

Cross Training

Everyone has his day and some days last longer than others.

Cross Training

There is no such thing as bad weather, only different kinds of good weather.

Cross Training

Men need some kind of external activity because they are inactive within.

Cross Training

The hardest thing to understand in the world is the income tax.

Reverse Crunches

affirmative - negative
forward - backward
below - above

Clueless is not a synonym of the four other words.

Reverse Crunches

night - day
pagan - religious
shy - bold

Sunlight is not a synonym of the four other words.

Reverse Crunches
face up - avoid
remember - forget
tame - wild

Divinity is not a synonym of the four other words.

Reverse Crunches
prevent - permit
wise - foolish
handy - inconvenient

Wondering is not a synonym of the four other words.

Reverse Crunches
homozygous - heterozygous
break - repair
peace - war

Common is not a synonym of the four other words.

Reverse Crunches
harmony - dissonance
despair - hope
smooth - rough

Truth is not a synonym of the four other words.

Maxing Out

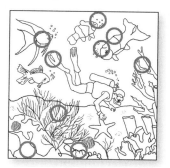

Maxing Out

Working the Memory Muscle
1. **Chacha**, **tutu**, and **step** are all words related to the theme "Dance."
2. **Sure-fire** is a compound word.
3. **Bathroom** comes first alphabetically on the list.
4. The word with the most letters is **nullification**.
5. **Gardening**, **hoover**, and **bathroom** are related to the theme "Home."

Working the Memory Muscle
1. There are four foreign words on the list: **negligee**, **aficionado**, **dolce vita**, and **baccarat**.
2. The two shortest words are **wit** and **liaison**.
3. **Baccarat** is a game.
4. **Poaching** and **turtleneck** are both in some way animal-related.

Can You Spot Me
Line 3, eighth from the right

Can You Spot Me
Line 4, fourth from the right

Can You Spot Me?
Line 5, fourth from the left

Can You Spot Me
Line 3, twelfth from the left

Can You Spot Me
Line 3, ninth from the left

Cooling Down
1. Wrong
2. Right
3. Right
4. Wrong
5. Wrong

Cooling Down
1. Right
2. Wrong
3. Wrong
4. Right
5. Right

Cooling Down
1. Right
2. Right
3. Wrong
4. Right
5. Right

Cooling Down
1. Wrong
2. Right
3. Wrong
4. Wrong
5. Right

No Pain, No _____
1. **Don't bite the hand** that feeds you.
2. Never **look a gift horse** in the mouth.
3. **Once bitten** twice shy.

No Pain, No _____
1. **Boys** will be boys.
2. **Bad news** travels fast.
3. **The hand that rocks the cradle** rules the world.

No Pain, No _____
1. **Don't judge a book** by its cover.
2. **No fool** like an old fool.
3. **Money** doesn't buy happiness.